W. H. Treacher

British Borneo

Sketches of Brunai, Sarawak, Labuan, and North Borneo

W. H. Treacher
British Borneo
Sketches of Brunai, Sarawak, Labuan, and North Borneo

ISBN/EAN: 9783337096298

Printed in Europe, USA, Canada, Australia, Japan

Cover: Foto ©Andreas Hilbeck / pixelio.de

More available books at **www.hansebooks.com**

BRITISH BORNEO:

SKETCHES OF
BRUNAI, SARAWAK, LABUAN,
AND
NORTH BORNEO...

BY

W. H. TREACHER, C.M.G., M.A. Oxon.,

Secretary to the Government of Perak,
Formerly Administrator of Labuan and H.B.M. Acting Consul-General in Borneo,
First Governor of British North Borneo.

Reprinted from the Journal of the Straits Settlements Branch
of the Royal Asiatic Society.

𝕾𝖎𝖓𝖌𝖆𝖕𝖔𝖗𝖊:
PRINTED AT THE GOVERNMENT PRINTING
DEPARTMENT.

1891.

TABLE OF CONTENTS.

CHAPTER I. PAGES 1–11.

The Hudson's Bay Company's Charter, 1670. British North Borneo Company's Charter, November 1881, as a territorial power. The example followed by Germany. Borneo the second largest island in the world. Visited by Friar Odoric, 1322, by Berthema, 1503; but not generally known until, in 1518 Portuguese, and in 1521 Spanish, expeditions touched there. Report of Pigafetta, the companion of Magellan, who found there a Chinese trading community. Origin of the name Borneo; sometimes known as Kalamantan. Spanish attack on Brunai, 1573. First Dutch connection, 1600; first British connection, 1609. Diamonds. Factory established by East India Company at Banjermassin, 1702, expelled by natives. British capture of Manila, 1762, and acquisition of Balambangan, followed by cession of Northern Borneo and part of Palawan. Spanish claims to Borneo abandoned by Protocol, 1885. Factory established at Balambangan, 1771, expelled by Sulus, 1775; re-opened 1803 and abandoned the following year. Temporary factory at Brunai. Pepper trade. Settlement of Singapore, 1819. Attracted trade of Borneo, Celebes, &c. Pirates. Brooke acquired Sarawak 1840, the first permanent British possession. Labuan a British Colony, 1846. The Dutch protest. Their possessions in Borneo. Spanish claims. Concessions of territory acquired by Mr. Dent, 1877-78. The monopolies of the first Europeans ruined trade: better prospect now opening. United States connection with Borneo. Population. Malays, their Mongolian origin. Traces of a Caucasic race, termed Indonesians. Buludupih legend. Names of aboriginal tribes. Pagans and Mahomedans.

CHAPTER II. PAGES 11–33.

Description of Brunai, the capital, and its river. Not a typical Malayan river. Spanish Catholic Mission. British Consulate. Inche Mahomed. Moses and a former American Consulate. Pigafetta's estimate of population in 1521, 150,000. Present estimate, 12,000. Decay of Brunai since British connection. Life of a Brunai noble; of the children; of the women. Modes of acquiring slaves: 'forced trade.' Condition of slaves. Character and customs of Brunai Malays. Their religion, gambling, cock-fighting: *amoks*, marriage. Sultan and ministers and officers of the state. How paid. Feudal rights—Ka-rájahan, Kouripan, Pusaka. Ownership of land. Modes of taxation. Laws. Hajis. Punishments. Executions. A naval officer's mistake. No army, navy, or police, but the people universally armed. Cannon foundries. Brass guns as currency. Dollars and copper coinage. Taxation. Revenue; tribute from Sarawak and North Borneo; coal resources.

CHAPTER III. PAGES 33-62.

Pigafetta's description of Brunai in 1521. Elephants. Reception by the King. Use of spirituous liquors. Population. Floating Market. Spoons. Ladies appearing in public. Obeisance. Modes of addressing nobles. The use of yellow confined to the Royal Family. Umbrellas closed when passing the Palace. Nobles only can sit in the stern of a boat. Ceremonies at a Royal reception; bees-wax candles.

Mr. Dalrymple's description of Brunai in 1884. Quakers' meeting. Way to a Malay's heart lies through his pocket. Market place and hideous women. Beauties of the Harems. Present population. Cholera. Exports. Former Chinese pepper plantations. Good water supply. Nobles corrupt; lower classes not. The late Sultan Mumim. The present Sultan. Kampongs, or parishes and guilds. Methods of fishing: Kèlongs; Rambat; peculiar mode of prawn-catching; Serambau; Pukat; hook and line; tuba fishing. Sago. Tobacco; its growth and use. Areca-nut; its use and effects. Costumes of men and women. Jewellery. Weapons. The *kris; parang; bliong; parang ilang*. The Kayans imitated by the Dyaks in a curious personal adornment. Canoes: dug-outs; *pakerangan;* prahus; tongkangs; steering gear; similarity to ancient Vikings' boat; boat races. Paddling. The Brunais teetotallers and temperate. Business and political negotiations transacted through agents. Time no object. The place of signatures taken by seals or *chops*. The great seal of state. Brunais styled by the aborigines, *Orang Abai*. By religion Mahomedans, but Pagan superstitions cling to them; instances. Traces of Javanese and Hindu influences. A native chronicle of Brunai; Mahomedanism established about 1478; connection of Chinese with Borneo; explanation of the name Kina-balu applied to the highest mountain in the island. Pepper planting by Chinese in former years. Mention of Brunai in Chinese history. Tradition of an expedition by Kublai Khan. The Chinese driven away by misgovernment. Their descendants in the Bundu district. Other traces of Chinese intercourse with Borneo. Their value as immigrants. European expeditions against Brunai. How Rajah Brooke acquired Sarawak amidst the roar of cannon. Brooke's heroic disinterestedness. His appointment as

TABLE OF CONTENTS. v

British confidential agent in Borneo. The episode of the murder of Rajah Muda Hassim and his followers. Brunai attacked by Admiral Sir Thomas Cochrane. Captain Rodney Mundy follows the Sultan into the jungle. The batteries razed and peace proclaimed.

CHAPTER IV. PAGES 63–77.

Sarawak under the Brooke dynasty. By incorporation of other rivers extends over 40,000 square miles, coast line 380 miles, population 280,000. Limbang annexed by Sarawak. Further extension impossible. The Trusan river; 'trowser wearers'; acquired by Sarawak. The Limbang, the rice pot of Brunai. The Cross flown in the Muhamadan capital by pagan savages. A launch decorated with skulls. Dyak militia, the Sarawak 'Rangers,' and native police force. Peace of Sarawak kept by the people. Cheap government. Absolute Monarchy. Nominated Councils. The 'Civil Service,' 'Residents.' Law, custom, equity and common sense. Slavery abolished. Sources of revenue—'Opium Farm' monopoly, poll tax, customs, excise, fines and fees. Revenue and expenditure. Early financial straits. Sarawak offered to England, France and Holland. The Borneo Company (Ltd.). Public debt. Advantages of Chinese immigration— 'Without the Chinese we can do nothing.' Java an exception. Chinese are good traders, agriculturists, miners, artizans, &c.: sober and law-abiding. Chinese secret societies and faction fights; death penalty for membership. Insurrection of Chinese, 1857. Chinese pepper and gambier planters. Exports—sago and jungle produce. Minerals—antimony, cinnabar, coal. Trade—agriculture. Description of the capital—Kuching. Sir Henry Keppel and Sir James Brooke. Piracy. 'Head money.' Charges against Sir J. Brooke. Recognition of Sarawak by United States and England. British protectorate. Death of Sir J. Brooke. Protestant and Roman Catholic Missions. Bishops MacDougal and Hose. Father Jackson. Mahomedans' conversion not attempted.

CHAPTER V. PAGES 77–84.

Incident of the Limbang rebellion against Sultan of Brunai. Oppression of the nobles. Irregular taxation—Chukei basoh batis, bongkar sauh, tulongan, chop bibas, &c. The orang kayas. Repulse of the Tummonggong. Brunai threatened. Intervention of the writer as acting Consul General. Datu Klassi. Meeting broken up on news of attack by Muruts. Sultan's firman eventually accepted. Demonstration by H.M.S. *Pegasus*. 'Cooking heads' in Brunai river. Death of Sultan Mumim. Conditions of firman not observed by successor. Sir Frederick Weld visits and reports on North Borneo and Brunai. Legitimate extension of Sarawak to be encouraged.

CHAPTER VI. PAGES 84-92.

The Colony of Labuan, ceded to England in return for assistance against pirates. For similar reasons monopoly of pepper trade granted to the East India Company in 1774. First British connection with Labuan in 1775, on expulsion from Balambangan. Belcher and Brooke visit Brunai, 1844, to enquire into alleged detention of an European female. Offer of cession of Labuan. Rajah Muda Hassim. At Sultan's request, British attack Osman, in Marudu Bay, 1845. Brooke recognised as the Queen's agent in Borneo. Captain Mundy, R.N., under Lord Palmerston's instructions, hoists British flag in Labuan, 24th Dec., 1846. Brooke appointed the first Governor, 1847, being at the same time British representative in Borneo, and independent ruler of Sarawak. His staff of 'Queen's officers'; concluded present treaty with Brunai; ceased to be Governor 1851. Sir Hugh Low, Sir J. Pope Hennessy, Sir Henry Bulwer, Sir Charles Lees. Original expecttations of the Colony not realized. Description of the island. The Kadayans. Agriculture, timber, trade. Overshadowed by Singapore, Sarawak, and North Borneo. Writer's suggestion for proclaiming British Protectorate over North Borneo, and assigning to it the Government of Labuan, has been adopted. Population of Labuan. Its coal measures and the failure of successive companies to work them; now being worked by Central Borneo Company (Ltd.). Chinese and natives worked well under Europeans. Revenue and expenditure. Labuan self-supporting since 1860. High-sounding official titles. One officer plays many parts. Labuan celebrated for its fruits, introduced by Sir Hugh Low. Sir Hugh's influence; instance of, when writer was fired on by Sulus. H.M.S. *Frolic* on a rock. Captain Buckle, R.N. Dr. Treacher's coco-nut plantation. The Church.

CHAPTER VII. PAGES 92-103.

British North Borneo; mode of acquisition; absence of any real native government; oppression of the inland pagans by the coast Muhamadans. Failure of American syndicate's Chinese colonization scheme in 1865. Colonel Torrey interests Baron Overbeck in the American concessions; Overbeck interests Sir Alfred Dent, who commissions him to acquire a transfer of the concessions from the Sultans of Brunai and Sulu, 1877-78. The ceded territory known as Sabah. Meaning of the term. Spanish claims on ground of suzerainty over Sulu. Not admitted by the British Government. The writer ordered to protest against Spanish claims to North Borneo, 1879. Spain renounced claims, by Protocol, 1885. Holland, on ground of the Treaty of 1824, objected to a British settlement in Borneo; also disputed the boundary between Dutch and British Borneo. The writer 'violates'

TABLE OF CONTENTS.   vii

Netherland territory and hoists the Company's flag on the south bank of the Siboku, 1883. Annual tribute paid to the Brunai Government. Certain intervening independent rivers still to be acquired. Dent's first settlements at Sandakan, Tampassuk, and Pappar. Messrs. Pryer, Pretyman, Witti, and Everett. Opposition of Datu Bahar at Pappar. Difficult position of the pioneer officers. Respect for Englishmen inspired by Brooke's exploits. Mr. W. H. Read. Mr. Dent forms a 'Provisional Association' pending grant of a Royal Charter, 1881, composed of Sir Rutherford Alcock, A. Dent, R. B. Martin, Admiral Mayne, W. H. Read. Sir Rutherford energetically advocates the scheme from patriotic motives. The British North Borneo Company incorporated by Royal Charter, 1st November, 1881; nominal capital two millions, £20 shares. 33,030 shares issued. Powers and conditions of the Charter. Flag.

CHAPTER VIII. PAGES 103-117.

Area of British North Borneo exceeds that of Ceylon; points of similarity; styled 'The New Ceylon.' Joseph Hatton's book. Tobacco planters attracted from Sumatra. Coast-line, harbours, stations. Sandakan town and harbour; founded by Mr. Pryer. Destroyed by fire. Formerly used as a blockade station by Germans trading with Sulu. Capture of the blockade runner *Sultana* by the Spaniards. Rich virgin soil and fever. Owing to propinquity of Hongkong and Singapore, North Borneo cannot become an emporium for eastern trade. Its mineralogical resources not yet ascertained. Gold, coal, and other minerals known to exist. Gold on the Segama river. Rich in timber. 'Billian' or ironwood; camphor. Timber Companies. On board one of Her Majesty's ships billian proved three times as durable as lignum vitæ. Mangrove forests. Monotony of tropical scenery. Trade—a list of exports. Edible birds'-nests. Description of the great Gomanton birds'-nests caves. Mr. Bampfylde. Bats' Guano. Mode of collecting nests. Lady and Miss Brassey visit the Madai caves, 1887. Bêche-de-mer, shark fins, cuttle fish. Position of Sandakan on the route between Australia and China—importance as a possible naval station. Shipping. Postal arrangements. Coinage. Currency. Banking. Probable cable station.

CHAPTER IX. PAGES 117-127.

Importance of the territory as a field for the cultivation of the fine tobacco used for 'wrappers.' Profits of Sumatra Tobacco Companies. Climate and Soil. Rainfall. Seasons. Dr. Walker. The sacred mountain, Kina-balu. Description of tobacco cultivation. Chinese the most suitable labour for tobacco; difficulty

viii   TABLE OF CONTENTS.

in procuring sufficient coolies. Count Geloes d'Elsloo. Coolies protected by Government. Terms on which land can be acquired. Tobacco export duty. Tobacco grown and universally consumed by the natives. Fibre plants. Government experimental garden. Sappan-wood. Cotton flock.

CHAPTER X. PAGES 127-147.

Erroneous ideas as to the objects of the Company. Difficult to steal Highlanders' trowsers. Natives 'take no thought for the morrow.' The Company does not engage in trade or agriculture. The Company's capital is a loan to the country, to be repaid with interest as the country developes under its administration. Large area of land to be disposed of without encroaching on native rights. Land sales regulations. Registration of titles. Minerals reserved. Tranfer from natives to foreigners effected through the Government. Form of Government—the Governor, Residents, &c. Laws and Proclamations. The Indian Penal, Criminal, and Civil procedure codes adopted. Slavery—provision in the Charter regarding. Slave legislation by the Company. Summary of Mr. Witti's report on the slave system. Messrs. Everett and Pryer's reports. Commander Edwards, R.N., attacks the kidnapping village of Teribas in H.M.S. *Kestrel*. Slave keeping no longer pays. Religious customs of the natives preserved by the Charter. Employment of natives as Magistrates, &c. Head-hunting. Audit of 'Heads Account.' Human sacrifices. Native punishments for adultery and theft. Causes of scanty population. Absence of powerful warlike tribes. Head hunting—its origin. An incident in Labuan. Mr. A. Cook. Mr. Jesse's report on the Muruts to the East India Company. Good qualities of the aborigines. Advice to young officers. The Muhamadans of the coast, the Brunais, Sulus, Bajows. Capture by Bajows of a boat from an Austrian frigate. Baron Oesterreicher. Gambling and cattle lifting. The independent intervening rivers. Fatal affray in the Kawang river: death of de Fontaine, Fraser and others. Mr. Little. Mr. Whitehead. Bombardment of Bajow villages by Captain A. K. Hope, R.N., H.M.S. *Zephyr*. Captain Alington, R.N., in H.M.S. *Satellite*. The Illanuns and Balinini. Absence of Negritos. The 'tailed' people. Desecration of European graves. Muhamadans' sepulture. Burial customs of the aborigines.

CHAPTER XI. PAGES 147-165.

Importance of introducing Chinese into Borneo. Java not an example. Sir Walter Medhurst Commissioner of Chinese immigration. The Hakka Chinese settlers. Sir Spencer St. John on Chinese immigration. The revenue and expenditure of the territory. Zeal of the Company's officers. Armed Sikh and Dyak police. Impossible to raise a native force. Heavy expenditure necessary in the first instance. Carping critics. Cordial support from Sir Cecil Clementi Smith and the Government of the Straits Settlements. Visit of Lord Brassey—his article in the 'Nineteenth Century.' Further expenditure for roads, &c., will be necessary. What the Company has done for Borneo. Geographical exploration. Witti and Hatton. The lake struck off the map. Witti's murder. Hatton's accidental death. Admiral Mayne, C.B. The *Sumpitan* or Blow-pipe. Errors made in opening most colonies, e.g. the Straits Settlements. The future of the country. The climate not unhealthy as a rule. Ladies. Game. No tigers. Crocodiles. The native dog. Pig and deer. Wild cattle. Elephants and Rhinoceros. Bear. Orang-utan. Long-nosed ape. Pheasants. The Company's motto—*Pergo et perago*. Governor Creagh. Mr. Kindersley.

ERRATUM.

Page 136, line 15, *for* 'head of a thief' *read* 'hand of a thief.'

BRITISH BORNEO:
SKETCHES OF
BRUNAI, SARAWAK, LABUAN
AND
NORTH BORNEO.

Chapter I.

IN 1670 CHARLES II granted to the Hudson's Bay Company a Charter of Incorporation, His Majesty delegating to the Company actual sovereignty over a very large portion of British North America, and assigning to them the exclusive monopoly of trade and mining in the territory. Writing in 1869, Mr. WILLIAM FORSYTH, Q.C., says:—" I have endeavoured to give an account of the constitution and history of the *last* of the great proprietary companies of England, to whom a kind of delegated authority was granted by the Crown. It was by some of these that distant Colonies were founded, and one, the most powerful of them all, established our Empire in the East and held the sceptre of the Great Mogul. But they have passed away

——fuit Ilium et ingens
Gloria Teucrorum—

and the Hudson's Bay Company will be no exception to the rule. It may continue to exist as a Trading Company, but as a Territorial Power it must make up its mind to fold its (buffalo) robes round it and die with dignity." Prophesying is hazardous work. In November, 1881, two hundred and eleven years after the Hudson's Bay Charter, and twelve years after the date of Mr. FORSYTH's article, Queen VICTORIA granted a Charter of Incorporation to the British North Borneo Company, which, by confirming the grants and concesssions acquired from the Sultans of Brunai and Sulu, constitutes the Company the sovereign ruler over a territory of 31,000 square miles, and, as the permission to trade, included in the Charter, has not been taken advantage of, the British North Borneo Company now does actually exist " as a Territorial Power " and not "as a Trading Company."

Not only this, but the example has been followed by Prince BISMARCK, and German Companies, on similar lines, have been incorporated by their Government on both coasts of Africa and in the Pacific; and another British Company, to operate on the Niger River Districts, came into existence by Royal Charter in July, 1886.

It used to be by no means an unusual thing to find an educated person ignorant not only of Borneo's position on the map, but almost of the very existence of the island which, regarding Australia as a continent, and yielding to the claims recently set up by New Guinea, is the second largest island in the world, within whose limits could be comfortably packed England, Scotland, Wales and Ireland, with a sea of dense jungle around them, as WALLACE has pointed out. Every school-board child now, however, knows better than this.

Though Friar ODORIC is said to have visited it about 1322, and LUDOVICO BERTHEMA, of Bologna, between 1503 and 1507, the existence of this great island, variously estimated to be from 263,000 to 300,000 square miles in extent, did not become generally known to Europeans until, in 1518, the Portuguese LORENZO DE GOMEZ touched at the city of Brunai. He was followed in 1521 by the Spanish expedition, which under the leadership of the celebrated Portuguese circum-navigator MAGELLAN, had discovered the Philippines, where, on the island of Mactan, their leader was killed in April, 1520. An account of the voyage was written by PIGAFETTA, an Italian volunteer in the expedition, who accompanied the fleet to Brunai after MAGELLAN's death, and published a glowing account of its wealth and the brilliancy of its Court, with its royally caparisoned elephants, a report which it is very difficult to reconcile with the present squalid condition of the existing "Venice of Hovels," as it has been styled from its palaces and houses being all built in, or rather over, the river to which it owes its name.

The Spaniards found at Brunai Chinese manufactures and Chinese trading junks, and were so impressed with the importance of the place that they gave the name of Borneo—a corruption of the native name Brunai—to the whole island, though the inhabitants themselves know no such general title for their country.

In some works, Pulau Kalamantan, which would signify *wild mangoes island,* is given as the native name for Borneo, but it is quite unknown, at any rate throughout North Borneo, and the island is by no means distinguished by any profusion of wild mangoes.*

In 1573, a Spanish Embassy to Brunai met with no very favourable reception, and three years later an expedition from Manila attacked the place and, deposing a usurping Sultan, re-instated his brother on the throne, who, to shew his gratitude, declared his kingdom tributary to Spain.

The Portuguese Governor of the Moluccas, in 1526, claimed the honour of being the first discoverer of Borneo, and this nation appears to have carried on trade with some parts of the island till they were driven out of their Colonies by the Dutch in 1609. But neither the Portuguese nor the Spaniards seem to have made any decided attempt to gain a footing in Borneo, and it is not until the early part of the 17th century that we find the two great rivals in the eastern seas—the English and the Dutch East India Trading Companies—turning their attention to the island. The first Dutchman to visit Borneo was OLIVER VAN NOORT, who anchored at Brunai in December, 1600, but though the Sultan was friendly, the natives made an attempt to seize his ship, and he sailed the following month, having come to the conclusion that the city was a nest of rogues.

---

* The explanation *Sago Island* has been given, *lamantah* being [the native term for the raw sago sold to the factories.

The first English connection with Borneo was in 1609, when trade was opened with Sukadana, diamonds being said to form the principal portion of it.

The East India Company, in 1702, established a Factory at Banjermassin, on the South Coast, but were expelled by the natives in 1706. Their rivals, the Dutch, also established Trading Stations on the South and South-West Coasts.

In 1761, the East India Company concluded a treaty with the Sultan of Sulu, and in the following year an English Fleet, under Admiral DRAKE and Sir WILLIAM DRAPER captured Manila, the capital of the Spanish Colony of the Philippines. They found in confinement there a Sultan of Sulu who, in gratitude for his release, ceded to the Company, on the 12th September, 1762, the island of Balambangan, and in January of the following year Mr. DALRYMPLE was deputed to take possession of it and hoist the British flag. Towards the close of 1763, the Sultan of Sulu added to his cession the northern portion of Borneo and the southern half of Palawan, together with all the intermediate islands. Against all these cessions the Spanish entered their protest, as they claimed the suzerainty over the Sulu Archipelago and the Sulu Dependencies in Borneo and the islands. This claim the Spaniards always persisted in, until, on the 7th March, 1885, a Protocol was entered into by England and Germany and Spain, whereby Spanish supremacy over the Sulu Archipelago was recognised on condition of their abandoning all claim to the portions of Northern Borneo which are now included in the British North Borneo Company's concessions.

In November, 1768, the Court of Directors in London, with the approval of Her Majesty's Ministers, who promised to afford protection to the new Colony, issued orders to the authorities at Bombay for the establishment of a settlement at Balambangan with the intention of diverting to it the China trade, of drawing to it the produce of the adjoining countries, and of opening a port for the introduction of spices, etc. by the Bugis, and for the sale of Indian commodities. The actual date of the foundation of the settlement is not known, but Mr. F. C. DANVERS states that in 1771 the Court ordered that the Government should be vested in "a chief and two other persons of Council," and that the earliest proceedings extant are dated Sulu, 1773, and relate to a broil in the streets between Mr. ALCOCK, the second in the Council, and the Surgeon of the *Britannia*.

This was a somewhat unpropitious commencement, and in 1774 the Court are found writing to Madras, to which Balambangan was subordinate, complaining of the "imprudent management and profuse conduct" of the Chief and Council.

In February, 1775, Sulu pirates surprised the stockade, and drove out the settlers, capturing booty valued at about a million dollars. The Company's officials then proceeded to the island of Labuan, now a British Crown Colony, and established a factory, which was maintained but for a short time, at Brunai itself. In 1803 Balambangan was again occupied, but as no commercial advantage accrued, it was abandoned in the following year, and so ended all attempts on the part of the East India Company to establish a Colony in Borneo.

While at Balambangan, the officers, in 1774, entered into negotiations with the Sultan of Brunai, and, on undertaking to protect him against Sulu and Mindanau pirates, acquired the exclusive trade in all the pepper grown in his country.

The settlement of Singapore, the present capital of the Straits Settlements, by Sir STAMFORD RAFFLES, under the orders of the East India Company in 1819, again drew attention to Borneo, for that judiciously selected and free port soon attracted to itself the trade of the Celebes, Borneo and the surrounding countries, which was brought to it by numerous fleets of small native boats. These fleets were constantly harassed and attacked and their crews carried off into slavery by the Balinini, Illanun, and Dyak pirates infesting the Borneo and Celebes coasts, and the interference of the British Cruisers was urgently called for and at length granted, and was followed, in the natural course of events, by political intervention, resulting in the brilliant and exciting episode whereby the modern successor of the olden heroes—Sir JAMES BROOKE—obtained for his family, in 1840, the kingdom of Sarawak, on the west coast of the island, which he in time purged of its two plague spots—head-hunting on shore, and piracy and slave-dealing afloat—and left to his heir, who has worthily taken up and carried on his work, the unique inheritance of a settled Eastern Kingdom, inhabited by the once dreaded head-hunting Dyaks and piratical Mahomedan Malays, the government of whom now rests absolutely in the hands of its one paternally despotic white ruler, or Rája. Sarawak, although not yet formally proclaimed a British Protectorate,* may thus be deemed the first permanent British possession in Borneo. Sir JAMES BROOKE was also employed by the British Government to conclude, on 27th May, 1847, a treaty with the Sultan of Brunai, whereby the cession to us of the small island of Labuan, which had been occupied as a British Colony in December, 1846, was confirmed, and the Sultan engaged that no territorial cession of any portion of his country should ever be made to any Foreign Power without the sanction of Great Britain.

These proceedings naturally excited some little feeling of jealousy in our Colonial neighbours—the Dutch—who ineffectually protested against a British subject becoming the ruler of Sarawak, as a breach of the tenor of the treaty of London of 1824, and they took steps to define more accurately the boundaries of their own dependencies in such other parts of Borneo as were still open to them. What we now call British North Borneo, they appear at that time to have regarded as outside the sphere of their influence, recognising the Spanish claim to it through their suzerainty, already alluded to, over the Sulu Sultan.

With this exception, and that of the Brunai Sultanate, already secured by the British Treaty, and Sarawak, now the property of the BROOKE family, the Dutch have acquired a nominal suzerainty over the whole of the rest of Borneo, by treaties with the independent rulers—an area comprising about two-thirds of the whole island, probably not a tenth part of which is under their actual direct administrative control.

---

* A British Protectorate was established over North Borneo on the 12th May, over Sarawak on the 14th June, and over Brunai on the 17th September, 1888. *Vide* Appendix.

They appear to have been so pre-occupied with the affairs of their important Colony of Java and its dependencies, and the prolonged, exhausting and ruinously expensive war with the Achinese in Sumatra, that beyond posting Government Residents at some of the more important points, they have hitherto done nothing to attract European capital and enterprise to Borneo, but it would now seem that the example set by the British Company in the North is having its effect, and I hear of a Tobacco Planting Company and of a Coal Company being formed to operate on the East Coast of Dutch Borneo.

The Spanish claim to North Borneo was a purely theoretical one, and not only their claim, but that also of the Sulus through whom they claimed, was vigorously disputed by the Sultans of Brunai, who denied that, as asserted by the Sulus, any portion of Borneo had been ceded to them by a former Sultan of Brunai, who had by their help defeated rival claimants and been seated on the throne. The Sulus, on their side, would own no allegiance to the Spaniards, with whom they had been more or less at war for almost three centuries, and their actual hold over any portion of North Borneo was of the slightest. Matters were in this position when Mr. ALFRED DENT, now Sir ALFRED DENT, K.C.M.G., fitted out an expedition, and in December, 1877, and January, 1878, obtained from the Sultans of Brunai and Sulu, in the manner hereafter detailed, the sovereign control over the North portion of Borneo, from the Kimanis river on the West to the Siboku river on the East, concessions which were confirmed by Her Majesty's Royal Charter in November, 1881.

I have now traced, in brief outline, the political history of Borneo from the time when the country first became generally known to Europeans—in 1518—down to its final division between Great Britain and the Netherlands in 1881.

If we can accept the statements of the earlier writers, Borneo was in its most prosperous stage before it became subjected to European influences, after which, owing to the mistaken and monopolising policy of the Commercial Companies then holding sway in the East, the trade and agriculture of this and other islands of the Malay Archipelago received a blow from which at any rate that of Borneo is only now recovering. By the terms of its Charter, the British North Borneo Company is prohibited from creating trade monopolies, and of its own accord it has decided not to engage itself in trading transactions at all, and as Rája BROOKE'S Government is similar to that of a British Crown Colony, and the Dutch Government no longer encourage monopolies, there is good ground for believing that the wrong done is being righted, and that a brighter page than ever is now being opened for Borneo and its natives.

Before finishing with this part of the subject, I may mention that the United States Government had entered into a treaty with the Sultan of Brunai, in almost exactly the same words as the English one, including the clause prohibiting cessions of territory without the consent of the other party to the treaty, and, in 1878, Commodore SCHUFELDT was ordered by his Government to visit Borneo and report on the cessions obtained by Mr. DENT. I was Acting British Consul-General at the time, and before leaving the Commodore informed me emphatically that he could discover no American interests in Borneo, "neither white nor black."

The native population of Borneo is given in books of reference as between 1,750,000 and 2,500,000. The aborigines are of the Malay race, which itself is a variety of the Mongolian and indeed, when inspecting prisoners, I have often been puzzled to distinguish the Chinese from the Malay, they being dressed alike and the distinctive *pig-tail* having been shaved off the former as part of the prison discipline.

These Mongolian Malays from High Asia, who presumably migrated to the Archipelago *viâ* the Malay Peninsula and Sumatra, must, however, have found Borneo and other of the islands partially occupied by a Caucasic race, as amongst the aborigines are still found individuals of distinctive Caucasic type, as has been pointed out to be the case with the Buludupih tribe of British North Borneo, by Dr. MONTANO, whom I had the pleasure of meeting in Borneo in 1878-9. To these the name of pre-Malays has been given, but Professor KEANE, to whom I beg to acknowledge my indebtedness on these points, prefers the title of Indonesians. The scientific descriptions of a typical Malay is as follows :—" Stature little over five feet, complexion olive yellow, head brachy-cephalous or round, cheek-bones prominent, eyes black and slighlty oblique, nose small but not flat, nostrils dilated, hands small and delicate, legs thin and weak, hair black, coarse and lank, beard absent or scant ; " but these Indonesians to whom belong most of the indigenous inhabitants of Celebes, are taller and have fairer or light brown complexions and regular features, connecting them with the brown Polynesians of the Eastern Pacific " who may be regarded as their descendants," and Professor KEANE accounts for their presence by assuming "a remote migration of the Caucasic race to South-Eastern Asia, of which evidences are not lacking in Camboja and elsewhere, and a further onward movement, first to the Archipelago and then East to the Pacific." It is needless to say that the aborigines themselves have the haziest and most unscientific notion of their own origin, as the following account, gravely related to me by a party of Buludupihs, will exemplify :—

" The Origin of the Buludupih Race."

In past ages a Chinese* settler had taken to wife a daughter of the aborigines, by whom he had a female child. Her parents lived in a hilly district (*Bulud*=hill), covered with a large forest tree, known by the name of *opih*. One day a jungle fire occurred, and after it was over, the child jumped down from the house (native houses are raised on piles off the ground), and went up to look at a half burnt *opih* log, and suddenly disappeared and was never seen again. But the parents heard the voice of a spirit issue from the log, announcing that it had taken the child to wife and that, in course of time, the bereaved parents would find an infant in the jungle, whom they were to consider as the offspring of the marriage,

---

* The Buludupihs inhabit the China or Kina-batangan river, and Sir HUGH Low, in a note to his history of the Sultans of Brunai, in a number of the Journal of the Straits Branch of the Royal Asiatic Society, says that it is probable that in former days the Chinese had a Settlement or Factory at that river, as some versions of the native history of Brunai expressly state that the Chinese wife of one of the earliest Sultans was brought thence.

and who would become the father of a new race. The prophecy of the spirit was in due time fulfilled."

It somewhat militates against the correctness of this history that the Buludupihs are distinguished by the absence of Mongolian features.

The general appellation given to the aborigines by the modern Malays—to whom reference will be made later on—is *Dyak,* and they are divided into numerous tribes, speaking very different dialects of the Malayo-Polynesian stock, and known by distinctive names, the origin of which is generally obscure, at least in British North Borneo, where these names are *not,* as a rule, derived from those of the rivers on which they dwell.

The following are the names of some of the principal North Borneo aboriginal tribes:—Kadaians, Dusuns, Ida'ans, Bisaias, Buludupihs, Eraans, Subans, Sun-Dyaks, Muruts, Tagaas. Of these, the Kadaians, Buludupihs, Eraans and one large section of the Bisaias have embraced the religion of Mahomet; the others are Pagans, with no set form of religion, no idols, but believing in spirits and in a future life, which they localise on the top of the great mountain of Kina-balu. These Pagans are a simple and more natural, less self-conscious, people than their Mahomedan brethren, who are ahead of them in point of civilization, but are more reserved, more proud and altogether less "jolly," and appear, with their religion, to have acquired also some of the characteristics of the modern or true Malays. A Pagan can sit, or rather squat, with you and tell you legends, or, perhaps, on an occasion join in a glass of grog, whereas the Mahomedan, especially the true Malay, looks upon the Englishman as little removed from a "Kafir"—an uncircumcised Philistine—who through ignorance constantly offends in minor points of etiquette, who eats pig and drinks strong drink, is ignorant of the dignity of repose, and whose accidental physical and political superiority in the present world will be more than compensated for by the very inferior and uncomfortable position he will attain in the next. The aborigines inhabit the interior parts of North Borneo, and all along the coast is found a fringe of true Malays, talking modern Malay and using the Arabic written character, whereas the aborigines possess not even the rudiments of an alphabet and, consequently, no literature at all.

How is the presence in Borneo of this more highly civilized product of the Malay race, differing so profoundly in language and manners from their kinsmen—the aborigines—to be accounted for? Professor KEANE once more comes to our assistance, and solves the question by suggesting that the Mongolian Malays from High Asia who settled in Sumatra, attained there a real national development in comparatively recent times, and after their conversion to Mahomedanism by the Arabs, from whom, as well as from the Bhuddist missionaries who preceded them, they acquired arts and an elementary civilization, spread to Borneo and other parts of Malaysia and quickly asserted their superiority over the less advanced portion of their race already settled there. This theory fits in well with the native account of the distribution of the Malay race, which makes Menangkabau, in Southern Sumatra, the centre whence they spread over the Malayan islands and peninsula.

The Professor further points out, that in prehistoric times the Malay and Indonesian stock spread westwards to Madagascar and eastwards to the Philippines and Formosa, Micronesia and Polynesia. "This astonishing expansion of the Malaysian people throughout the Oceanic area is sufficiently attested by the diffusion of common (Malayo-Polynesian) speech from Madagascar to Easter Island and from Hawaii to New Zealand."

CHAPTER II.

The headquarters of the true Malay in Northern Borneo is the City of Brunai, on the river of that name, on the North-West Coast of the island, where resides the Court of the only nominally independent Sultan now remaining in the Archipelago.*

The Brunai river is probably the former mouth of the Limbang, and is now more a salt water inlet than a river. Con-

---

* He has since been "protected"—see ante page 6, note.

trary, perhaps, to the general idea, an ordinary eastern river, at any rate until the limit of navigability for European craft is attained, is not, as a rule, a thing of beauty by any means.

The typical Malay river debouches through flat, fever-haunted swampy country, where, for miles, nothing meets the eye but the monotonous dark green of the level, interminable mangrove forest, with its fantastic, interlacing roots, whose function it appears to be to extend seaward, year by year, its dismal kingdom of black fetid mud, and to veil from the rude eye of the intruder the tropical charms of the country at its back. After some miles of this cheerless scenery, and at a point where the fresh water begins to mingle with the salt, the handsome and useful *nipa* palm, with leaves twenty to thirty feet in length, which supply the native with the material for the walls and roof of his house, the wrapper for his cigarette, the sugar for his breakfast table, the salt for his daily needs and the strong drink to gladden his heart on his feast days, becomes intermixed with the mangrove and finally takes its place—a pleasing change, but still monotonous, as it is so dense that, itself growing in the water, it quite shuts out all view of the bank and surrounding country.

One of the first signs of the fresh river water, is the occurrence on the bank of the graceful *nibong* palm, with its straight, slender, round stem, twenty to thirty feet in height, surmounted with a plume of green leaves. This palm, cut into lengths and requiring no further preparation, is universally employed by the Malay for the posts and beams of his house, always raised several feet above the level of the ground, or of the water, as the case may be, and, split up into lathes of the requisite size, forms the frame-work of the walls and roof, and constitutes the flooring throughout. With the pithy centre removed, the *nibong* forms an efficient aqueduct, in the absence of bambu, and its young, growing shoot affords a cabbage, or salad, second only to that furnished by the coconut, which will next come into view, together with the betel *(Areca)* nut palm, if the river visited is an inhabited one; but if uninhabited, the traveller will find nothing but thick, almost impenetrable jungle, with mighty trees shooting up one hundred to a hundred and fifty feet without a branch, in their endeavour to get their share of the sun-light, and supporting on their trunks and branches enormous creepers, rattans, graceful ferns and lovely orchids and other luxuriant epiphytal growths. Such is the typical North Borneo river, to which, however, the Brunai is a solitary exception. The mouth of the Brunai river is approached between pretty verdant islets, and after passing through a narrow and tortuous passage, formed naturally by sandbanks and artificially by a barrier of stones, bare at low water, laid down in former days to keep out the restless European, you find your vessel, which to cross the bar should not draw more than thirteen or fourteen feet, in deep water between green, grassy, hilly, picturesque banks, with scarcely a sign of the abominable mangrove, or even of the *nipa,* which, however, to specially mark the contrast formed by this stream, are both to be found in abundance in the *upper* portion of the river, which the steamer cannot enter. After passing a small village or two, the first object which used to attract attention was the brick ruins of a Roman Catholic Church, which had been erected here by the late Father CUARTERON, a Spanish Missionary of the Society of the Propaganda Fide, who, originally a jovial sea captain, had the good fortune to light upon a wrecked treasure ship in the Eastern seas, and, feeling presumably unwonted twinges of conscience, decided to devote the greater part of his wealth to the Church, in which he took orders, eventually attaining the rank of Prefect Apostolic. His Mission, unfortunately, was a complete failure, but though his assistants were withdrawn, he stuck to his post to the last and, no doubt, did a certain amount of good in liberating, from time to time, Spanish subjects he found in slavery on the Borneo Coast.

Had the poor fellow settled in the interior, amongst the Pagans, he might, by his patience and the example of his good life, have made some converts, but amongst the Mahomedans of the coast it was labour in vain. The bricks of his Brunai Church have since been sold to form the foundation of a steam sawmill.

Turning a sharp corner, the British Consulate is reached,

where presides, and flies with pride the Union Jack, Her Majesty's Consular Agent, Mr. or Inche MAHOMET, with his three wives and thirteen children. He is a native of Malacca and a clever, zealous, courteous and hospitable official, well versed in the political history of Brunai since the advent of Sir JAMES BROOKE.

The British is the only Consulate now established at Brunai, but once the stars and stripes proudly waved over the Consulate of an unpaid American Consul. There was little scope at Brunai for a white man in pursuit of the fleeting dollar, and one day the Consulate was burnt to the ground, and a heavy claim for compensation for this alleged act of incendiarism was sent in to the Sultan. His Highness disputed the claim, and an American man-of-war was despatched to make enquiries on the spot. In the end, the compensation claimed was not enforced, and Mr. MOSES, the Consul, was not subsequently, I think, appointed to any other diplomatic or consular post by the President of the Republic. A little further on are the palaces, shops and houses of the city of Brunai, all, with the exception of a few brick shops belonging to Chinamen, built over the water in a reach where the river broadens out, and a vessel can steam up the High Street and anchor abreast of the Royal Palace. When PIGAFETTA visited the port in 1521, he estimated the number of houses at 25,000, which, at the low average of six to a house, would give Brunai a population of 150,000 people, many of whom were Chinese, cultivating pepper gardens, traces of which can still be seen on the now deserted hills. Sir SPENCER ST. JOHN, formerly H. B. M. Consul-General in Borneo, and who put the population at 25,000 at the lowest in 1863, asserts that fifteen is a fair average to assign to a Brunai house, which would make the population in PIGAFETTA'S time 375,000. From his enquiries he found that the highest number was seventy, in the Sultan's palace, and the lowest seven, in a fisherman's small hut. PIGAFETTA, however, probably alluded to families, *fires* I think is the word he makes use of, and more than one family is often found occupying a Brunai house. The present population perhaps does not number more than 12,000 or 15,000 natives, and about eighty Chinese and a few Kling shop-keepers, as natives of India are here styled. Writing in 1845, Sir JAMES BROOKE, then the Queen's first Commissioner to Brunai, says with reference to this Sultanate:—" Here the experiment may be fairly tried, on the smallest possible scale of expense, whether a beneficial European influence may not re-animate a falling State and at the same time extend our commerce. * * * If this tendency to decay and extinction be inevitable, if this approximation of European policy to native Government should be unable to arrest the fall of the Bornean dynasty, yet we shall retrieve a people already habituated to European habits and manners, industrious interior races; and if it become necessary, a Colony gradually formed and ready to our hand in a rich and fertile country," and elsewhere he admits that the regeneration of the Borneo Malays through themselves was a hobby of his. The experiment has been tried and, so far as concerns the re-animation of the Malay Government of Brunai, the verdict must be " a complete failure." The English are a practical race, and self-interest is the guide of nations in their intercourse with one another; it was not to be supposed that they would go out of their way to teach the degenerate Brunai aristocracy how to govern in accordance with modern ideas; indeed, the Treaty we made with them, by prohibiting, for instance, their levying customs duties, or royalties, on the export of such jungle products as gutta percha and India rubber, in the collection of which the trees yielding them are entirely destroyed, and by practically suggesting to them the policy, or rather the impolicy, of imposing the heavy due of $1 per registered ton on all European Shipping entering their ports, whether in cargo or in ballast, scarcely tended to stave off their collapse, and the Borneans must have formed their own conclusions from the fact that when they gave up portions of their territory to the BROOKES and to the British North Borneo Company, the British Government no longer called for the observance of these provisions of the Treaty in the ceded districts. The English have got all they wanted from Brunai, but I think it can scarcely be said that they have done very much for it in return. I remember that the late Sultan thought it an inexplicable thing that we could not assist him to recover a debt due to him by one of the British Coal Companies which tried their luck in Borneo. Moreover, even the cession to their good and noble friend Sir JAMES BROOKE of the Brunai Province of Sarawak has been itself also, to a certain extent, a factor in their Government's decay, that State, under the rule of the Rája—CHARLES BROOKE— having attained its present prosperous condition at the expense of Brunai and by gradually absorbing its territory.

Between British North Borneo, on the one side, and Sarawak, on the other, the sea-board of Brunai, which, when we first appeared on the scene, extended from Cape Datu to Marudu Bay—some 700 miles—is now reduced to 125 or 130 miles, and, besides the river on which it is built, Brunai retains but two others of any importance, both of which are in rebellion of a more or less vigorous character, and the whole State of Brunai is so sick that its case is now under the consideration of Her Majesty's Government.

Thus ends in collapse the history of the last independent Malay Government. Excepting only Johor (which is prosperous owing to its being under the wing of Singapore, which fact gives confidence to European and Chinese capitalists and Chinese labourers, and to its good fortune in having a wise and just ruler in its Sultan, who owes his elevation to British influences), all the Malay Governments throughout the Malay Archipelago and in the Malay Peninsula are now subject either to the English, the Dutch, the Spanish or the Portuguese. This decadence is not due to any want of vitality in the race, for under European rule the Malay increases his numbers, as witness the dense population of Java and the rapidly growing Malay population of the Straits Settlements.

That the Malay does so flourish in contact with the European and the Chinese is no doubt to some extent due to his attachment to the Mahomedan faith, which as a tee-total religion is, so far, the most suitable one for a tropical race ; it has also to be remembered that he inhabits tropical countries, where the white man cannot perform out-door labour and appears only as a Government Official, a merchant or a planter.

But the decay of the Brunai aristocracy was probably inevitable. Take the life of a young noble. He is the son of one of perhaps thirty women in his father's harem, his mother is entirely without education, can neither read nor write, is never allowed to appear in public or have any influence in public affairs, indeed scarcely ever leaves her house, and one of her principal excitements, perhaps, is the carrying on of an intrigue, an excitement enhanced by the fact that discovery means certain death to herself and her lover.

Brunai being a water town, the youngster has little or no chance of a run and game ashore, and any exercise he takes is confined to *being* paddled up and down the river in a canoe, for to paddle himself would be deemed much too degrading— a Brunai noble should never put his hand to any honest physical work—even for his own recreation. I once imported a Rob Roy canoe from England and amused myself by making long paddling excursions, and I would also sometimes, to relieve the monotony of a journey in a native boat, take a spell at the paddle with the men, and I was gravely warned by a native friend that by such action I was seriously compromising myself and lowering my position in the eyes of the higher class of natives. At an early age the young noble becomes an object of servile adulation to the numerous retainers and slaves, both male and female, and is by them initiated in vicious practices and, while still a boy, acquires from them some of the knowledge of a fast man of the world. As a rule he receives no sort of school education. He neither rides nor joins in the chase and, since the advent of Europeans, there have been no wars to brace his nerves, or call out any of the higher qualities of mind or body which may be latent in him; nor is there any standing army or navy in which he might receive a beneficial training. No political career, in the sense we attach to the term, is open to him, and he has no feelings of patriotism whatever. That an aristocracy thus nurtured should degenerate can cause no surprise. The general term for the nobles amongst the Brunais is *Pangeran,* and their numbers may be guessed when it is understood that every son and daughter of every many-wived noble is also a Pangeran.

Some of these unfortunate noblemen have nothing wherewith to support their position, and in very recent times I have actually seen a needy Pangeran, in a British Colony where he could not live by oppression or theft, driven to work in a coal mine or drive a buffalo cart.

With the ordinary freeborn citizen of Brunai life opens under better auspices. The children are left much to themselves and are merry, precocious, naked little imps, able to look out for themselves at a very much earlier age than is the case with European infants, and it is wonderful to see quite little babies clambering up the rickety stairs leading from the river to the house, or crawling unheeded on the tottering verandahs. Almost before they can walk they can swim, and they have been known to share their mother's cigarettes while still in arms. All day long they amuse themselves in miniature canoes, rolling over and over in the water, regardless of crocodiles. Happy children! they have no school and no clothes—one might, perhaps, exclaim happy parents, too! Malays are very kind and indulgent to their children and I do not think I have seen or heard of a case of the application of the parental hand to any part of the infant person. As soon as he is strong enough, say eight or nine years of age, the young Malay, according to the *kampong,* or division of the town, in which his lot has been cast, joins in his father's trade and becomes a fisherman, a trader, or a worker in brass or in iron as the case may be. The girls have an equally free and easy time while young, their only garments being a silver fig leaf, fastened to a chain or girdle round the waist. As they grow up they help their mothers in their household duties, or by selling their goods in the daily floating market; they marry young and are, as a rule, kindly treated by their husbands. Although Mahomedans, they can go about freely and unveiled, a privilege denied to their sisters of the higher classes. The greatest misfortune for such a girl is, perhaps, the possession of a pretty face and figure, which may result in her being honoured with the attentions of a noble, in whose harem she may be secluded for the rest of her life, and, as her charms wane her supply of both food and clothing is reduced to the lowest limit.

By the treaty with Great Britain traffic in slaves is put down, that is, Borneo is no longer the mart where, as in former days, the pirates can bring in their captives for sale; but the slaves already in the place have not been liberated, and a slave's children are slaves, so that domestic slavery, as it is termed, exists on a very considerable scale in Brunai. Slaves were acquired in the old days by purchase from pirates and, on any pretext, from the Pagan tribes of Borneo. For instance, if a feudal chief of an outlying river was in want of some cash, nothing was easier than for him to convict a man, who was the father of several children, of some imaginary offence, or neglect of duty, and his children, girls and boys, would be seized and carried off to Brunai as slaves. A favourite method was that of "forced trade." The chief would send a large quantity of trade goods to a Pagan village and leave them there to be sold at one hundred per cent. or more above their proper value, all legitimate trade being prohibited meanwhile, and if the money or barter goods were not forthcoming when demanded, the deficiency would be made up in slaves. This kind of oppression was very rife in the neighbourhood of the capital when I first became acquainted with Borneo in 1871, but the power of the chiefs has been much curtailed of late, owing to the extensive cessions of territory to Sarawak and the British North Borneo Company, and their hold on the rivers left to them has become very precarious, since the warlike Kyans passed under Rája BROOKE'S sway. This tribe, once the most powerful in Borneo, was always ready at the Sultan's call to raid on any tribe who had incurred his displeasure and revelled in the easy acquisition of fresh heads, over which to hold the triumphal dance. The Brunai Malays are not a warlike race, and the Rájas find that, without the Kyans, they are as a tiger with its teeth drawn and its claws pared, and the Pagan tribes have not been slow to make the discovery for themselves. Those on the Limbang river have been in open rebellion for the last three or four years and are crying out to be taken under the protection of the Queen, or, failing that, then under the " Kompani," as the British North Borneo Company's Government like that of the East India Company in days gone by, is styled, or under Sarawak.

The condition of the domestic slaves is not a particularly hard one unless, in the case of a girl, she is compelled to join the harem, when she becomes technically free, but really only changes one sort of servitude for another and more degrading one. With this exception, the slaves live on friendly terms with their masters' families, and the propinquity of a British Colony—Labuan—has tended to ameliorate their condition, as an ill-used slave can generally find means to escape thither and, so long as he remains there, he is a free man.

The scientific description of a typical Malay has already been given, and it answers well on almost all points for the Brunai specimen, except that the nose, as well as being small, is, in European eyes, deficient as to "bridge," and the legs cannot be described as weak, indeed the Brunai Malay, male and female, is a somewhat fleshy animal. In temperament, the Malay is described as "taciturn, undemonstrative, little given to outward manifestations of joy or sorrow, courteous towards each other, kind to their women and children. Not elated by good or depressed by bad fortune, but capable of excesses when roused. Under the influence of religious excitement, losses at gambling, jealousy or other domestic troubles they are liable to *amok* or run-a-muck, an expression which appears to have passed into the English language." With strangers, the Brunai Malay is doubtless taciturn, but I have heard Brunai ladies among themselves, while enjoying their betel-nut, rival any old English gossips over their cup of tea, and on an expedition the men will sometimes keep up a conversation long into the night till begged to desist. Courtesy seems to be innate in every Malay of whatever rank, both in their intercourse with one another and with strangers. The meeting at Court of two Brunai nobles who, perhaps, entertain feelings of the greatest hatred towards each other, is an interesting study, and the display of mutual courtesy unrivalled.

I need scarcely say that horseplay and practical joking are unknown, contradiction is rarely resorted to and "chaff" is only known in its mildest form. The lowest Malay will never pass in front of you if it can be avoided, nor hand anything to another across you. Unless in case of necessity, a Malay will not arouse his friend from slumber, and then only in the gentlest manner possible. It is bad manners to point at all, but, if it is absolutely necessary to do so, the forefinger is never employed, but the person or object is indicated, in a sort of shamefaced way, with the thumb. It is impolite to bare a weapon in public, and Europeans often show their ignorance of native etiquette by asking a Malay visitor to let them examine the blade of the *kris* he is wearing. It is not considered polite to enquire after the welfare of the female members of a Brunai gentleman's household. For a Malay to uncover his head in your presence would be an impertinence, but a guttural noise in his throat after lunching with you is a polite way of expressing pleased satisfaction with the excellence of the repast. This latter piece of etiquette has probably been adopted from the Chinese. The low social position assigned to women by Brunai Malays, as by nearly all Mahomedan races, is of course a partial set-off to the general courtesy that characterises them. The average intelligence of what may be called the working class Malay is almost as far superior to that, say, of the British country bumpkin as are his manners. Mr. H. O. FORBES says in his "Naturalist in the Eastern Archipelago" that he was struck with the natives' acute observation in natural history and the accuracy with which they could give the names, habits and uses of animals and plants in the jungle, and the traveller cannot but admire the general handiness and adapability to changed circumstances and customs and quickness of understanding of the Malay coolies whom he engages to accompany him.

Cannot one imagine the stolid surprise and complete obfuscation of the English peasant if an intelligent Malay traveller were to be suddenly set down in his district, making enquiries as to the, to him, novel forms of plants and animals and asking for minute information as to the manners and customs of the new people amongst whom he found himself, and, generally, seeking for information as the reasons for this and for that?

Their religion sits somewhat lightly on the Brunai Malays; the Mahomedan Mosque in the capital was always in a very dirty and neglected state, though prayers were said there daily, and I have never seen a Borneo Malay under the influence of religious excitement.

Gambling prevails, doubtless, and so does cock-fighting, but neither is the absorbing passion which it seems, from travellers' accounts, to be with Malays elsewhere.

When visiting the Spanish settlements in Sulu and Balabac, I was surprised to find regular officially licensed cock-fighting pits, with a special seat for the Spanish Governor, who was expected to be present on high days and holidays. I have never come across a regular cockpit in Brunai, or in any part of northern Borneo.

The *amoks* that I have been cognisant of have, consequently, not been due to either religious excitement, or to losses at gambling, but, in nearly every case, to jealousy and domestic trouble, and their occurrence almost entirely confined to the British Colony of Labuan where, of course, the Mahomedan pains and penalties for female delinquencies could not be enforced. I remember one poor fellow whom I pitied very much. He had good reason to be jealous of his wife and, in our courts, could not get the redress he sought. He explained to me that a mist seemed to gather before his eyes and that he became utterly unconscious of what he was doing—his will was quite out of his control. Some half dozen people—children, men and women—were killed, or desperately wounded before he was overpowered. He acknowledged his guilt, and suffered death at the hands of the hangman with quiet dignity. Many tragical incidents in the otherwise uneventful history of Labuan may be traced to the manner in which marriages are contracted amongst the Borneo Malays. Marriages of mere love are almost unknown; they are generally a matter of bargain between the girls' parents and the expectant bridegroom, or his parents, and, practically, everything depends on the amount of the dowry or *brihan*—literally " gift "—which the swain can pay to the former. In their own country there exist certain safeguards which prevent any abuse of this system, but it was found that under the English law a clever parent could manage to dispose of his daughter's hand several times over, so that really the plot of Mrs. CAMPBELL PRAED'S somewhat unpleasant play " Arianne " was anticipated in the little colony of Labuan. I was once called upon, as Coroner, to inquire into the deaths of a young man and his handsome young wife, who were discovered lying dead, side by side, on the floor of their house. The woman was found to be fearfully cut about; the man had but one wound, in his abdomen, penetrating the bowels. There was only one weapon by which the double murder could have been committed, a knife with a six inch blade, and circumstances seemed to point to the probability that the woman had first stabbed the man, who had then wrenched the knife from her grasp and hacked her to death. The man was not quite dead when found and he accused the dead woman of stabbing him. It was found, that they had not long been married and that, apparently with the girl's consent, her father had been negociating for her marriage with another. The father himself was subsequently the first man murdered in British North Borneo after the assumption of the Government by the Company, and his murderer was the first victim of the law in the new Colony. Altogether a tragical story.

Many years ago another *amok*, which was near being tragical, had an almost comical termination. The then Colonial Treasurer was an entertaining Irishman of rather mature age. Walking down to his office one day he found in the road a Malay hacking at his wife and another man. Home rule not being then in fashion with the Irish, the Treasurer, armed only with his sun umbrella, attempted to interfere, when the *amoker* turned furiously on him and the Irish official, who was of spare build, took to his heels and made good his escape, the chase, though a serious matter to him, causing irrepressible mirth to onlookers. The man was never captured, and his victims, though disfigured, recovered. I remember being struck by the contemptuous reply of Sir HUGH LOW'S Chinese servant when he warned him to be on his guard, as there was an *amoker* at large, and alluded to Mr. C.'S narrow escape—it was to the effect that the Treasurer was foolish to interfere in other people's concerns. This unwillingness to busy oneself in others' affairs, which sometimes has the appearance of callousness, is characteristic of Malays and Chinese.

The readers of a book of travels are somewhat under a disadvantage in forming their opinion of a country, in that incidents are focussed for them by those of the same nature being grouped together. I do not wish it to be thought that murders and *amoks* are at all common occurrences in Northern Borneo, indeed they are very few and far between, and criminal acts of all kinds are remarkably infrequent, that is, of course, if we regard head-hunting as an amusement sanctioned by usage, especially as, in the parts under native government, there is a total absence of any kind of police force, while every man carries arms, and houses with palm leaf walls and innocent of locks, bolts and bars, offer unusual temptations to the burglariously inclined. My wife and I nearly always slept without a watchman and with the doors and windows unclosed, the servants' offices being detached from the house, and we have never had any of our property stolen except by a " boy."

Brunai is governed by a Sultan styled Iang-di-pertuan, "he who rules," and four principal Ministers of State, "Wazirs"—the Pangeran Bandahara, the Pangeran di Gadong, the Pangeran Pamancha and the Pangeran Temenggong. These Ministers are generally men of the royal blood, and fly distinctive flags at their residences, that of the Bandahara being white, of the di Gadong, green, and of the Temenggong, red. The flags are remarkably simple and inexpensive, but quite distinctive, each consisting of a square bit of bunting or cloth of the requisite colour, with the exception of the Temenggong's, which is cut in the shape of a burgee. The Sultan's flag is a plain piece of yellow bunting, yellow being the Brunei royal colour, and no man, except the

Sovereign, is permitted to exhibit that colour in any portion of his dress. It shows how little importance attaches to the female sex that a lady, even a slave, can sport yellow in her dress, or any colour she chooses. Theoretically the duties of the Bandahara are those of a Home Secretary; the di Gadong is Keeper of the Seal and Chancellor of the Exchequer; the Pamancha's functions I am rather uncertain about, as the post has remained unfilled for many years past, but they would seem to partake of those of a Home Secretary; and the Temenggong is the War Minister and Military and Naval Commander-in-chief, and appears also to hear and decide criminal and civil cases in the city of Brunai. These appointments are made by the Sultan, and for life, but it will be understood that, in such a rough and ready system of government as that of Brunai, the actual influence of each Minister depends entirely on his own character and that of the Sultan. Sometimes one Minister will practically usurp the functions of some, or, perhaps, all the others, leaving them only their titles and revenues, while often, on a vacancy occurring, the Sultan does not make a fresh appointment, but himself appropriates the revenue of the office leaving the duties to take care of themselves.

To look after trade and commerce there is, in theory, an inferior Minister, the Pangeran Shabander.

There is another class of Ministers—*Mantri*—who are selected by the Sultan from among the people, and are chosen for their intelligence and for the influence and following they have amongst the citizens. They possess very considerable political power, their opinions being asked on important matters. Such are the two Juwatans and the Orang Kaya di Gadong, who may be looked upon as the principal officers of the Sultan and the Wazirs.

The State officials are paid by the revenues of certain districts which are assigned, as will be seen below, to the different offices.

The Mahomedan Malays, it has already been explained, were an invading and conquering race in Borneo, and their chiefs would seem to have divided the country, or, rather, the inhabitants, amongst themselves, in much the same way as England was parcelled out among the followers of WILLIAM THE CONQUEROR. The people of all the rivers* and of the interior, up to the limits where the Brunai Malays can enforce their authority, own as their feudal lord and pay taxes to either the Sultan, in his unofficial capacity, or to one of the nobles, or else they are attached to the office of Sultan or one of the great Ministers of State, and, again theoretically speaking, all the districts in the Sultanate are known, from the fact of the people on them belonging to a noble, or to the reigning Sultan for the time being, or to one of the Ministers of State, as either:—

1. Ka-rájahan—belonging to the Sultan or Rája.
or 2. Kouripan—belonging to certain public officials during their term of office.
or 3. Pusaka or Tulin—belonging to the Sultan or any of the nobles in their unofficial capacity.

The crown and the feudal chiefs did not assert any claim to the land; there are, for instance, no "crown lands," and, in the case of land not owned or occupied, any native could settle upon and cultivate it without payment of any rent or land tax, either to the Sultan or to the feudal chief of the district; consequently, land was comparatively little regarded, and what the feudal chief claimed was the people and not the land, so much so that, as pointed out by Mr. P. LEYS in a Consular report, in the case of the people removing from one river to another, they did not become the followers of the chief who owned the population amongst whom they settled, but remained subject to their former lord, who had the right of following them and collecting from them his taxes as before. It is only of quite recent years, imitating the example of the English in Labuan, where all the land was assumed to be the property of the Sovereign and leased to individuals for a term of years, that the nobles have, in some instances, put forward a claim to ownership of the land on which their followers

---

* Owing to the absence of roads and the consequent importance of rivers as means of getting about, nearly all districts in Borneo are named after their principal river.

chose to settle, and have endeavoured to pose as semi-independent princes. These feudal chiefs tax, or used to tax, their followers in proportion to their inability to resist their lords' demands. A poll tax, usually at the rate of $2 for married men and $1 for bachelors, is a form of taxation to which, in the absence of any land tax, no objection is made, but the chiefs had also the power of levying special taxes at their own sweet will, when they found their expenditure in excess of their income, and advantage was taken of any delay in payment of taxes, or of any breach of the peace, or act of theft occurring in a district, to impose excessive fines on the delinquents, all of which if paid went to the chief; and if the fine could not be paid, the defaulter's children might be seized and eventually sold into slavery. The system of "forced trade" I have alluded to when speaking on the subject of domestic slavery. The chiefs were all absentees and, while drawing everything they could out of their districts, did nothing for their wretched followers. The taxes were collected by their messengers and slaves, unscrupulous men who were paid by what they could get out of the people in excess of what they were bidden to demand, and who, while engaged in levying the contributions, lived at free quarters on the people, who naturally did their best to expedite their departure. Petty cases of dispute were settled by headmen appointed by the chief and termed *orang kaya*, literally "rich men." These *orang kayas* were often selected from their possessing some little property and being at the same time subservient to the chief. In many cases, it seemed to me, that they were chosen for their superior stupidity and pliability. I have made use of the past tense throughout my description of these feudal chiefs as, happily, for reasons already given, the "good old times" are rapidly passing away.

The laws of Brunai are, in theory, those inculcated by the Korán and there are one or two officials who have some slight knowledge of Mahomedan law. Owing to the cheap facilities offered by the numerous steamers at Singapore, there are many Hajis—that is, persons who have made the pilgrimage to Mecca—amongst the Brunais and the Kadaaans, amongst the latter more especially, but of course a visit to Mecca does not necessarily imply that the pilgrim has obtained any actual knowledge of the holy book, which some of them can decipher, the Malays having adopted the Arabic alphabet, but without, however, understanding the meaning of the Arabic words of which it consists. A friend of mine, son of the principal exponent of Mahomedan law in the capital, and who became naturalised as a British subject, had studied law in Constantinople.

There is no gaol in Brunai, and fines are found to be a more profitable mode of punishment than incarceration, the judge generally pocketing the fine, and when it does become necessary to keep an offender in detention, it is done by placing his feet in the stocks, which are set up on the public staging or landing before the reception room of the Sultan, or of one of his chief Ministers, and the wretched man may be kept there for months.

The punishment for theft, sanctioned by the Korán, is by cutting off the right hand, but this barbarous, though effective, penalty has been discountenanced by the English. On one occasion, however, when acting as H. B. M. Consul-General, I received my information too late to interfere. I had been on a visit to the late Sultan in a British gunboat, and anchored off the palace. During the evening, just before dinner, notwithstanding the watch kept on deck, some natives came alongside and managed to hook out through the ports my gold watch and chain from off the Captain's table, and the first Lieutenant's revolver from his cabin. During our interview next morning with the Sultan, I twitted him on the skill and daring of Brunai thieves, who could perpetrate a theft from a friendly war-ship before the windows of the Royal palace. The Sultan said nothing, but was evidently much annoyed, and a few weeks afterwards the revolver and the remains of my watch and chain were sent to me at Labuan, with a letter saying that three thieves had been punished by having had their hands chopped off. I subsequently heard that two of the unfortunate men had died from the effects of this cruel punishment.

On another occasion, some Brunai thieves skilfully dismounted and carried off two brass signal guns from the poop of a merchant steamer at anchor in the river, eluding the vigilance of the quarter-master, while the skipper and some of the officers were asleep on the skylight close by. The guns were subsequently recovered.

Execution is either by means of the bow string or the *kris*.

I had once the unpleasant duty of having to witness the execution by the bow string of a man named MAIDIN, as it was feared that, being the son of a favourite officer of the Sultan, the execution might be a sham one. This man, with others, had raided a small settlement of Chinese traders from Labuan on the Borneo coast, killing several of the shop-keepers and looting the settlement. So weak was the central government, and so little importance did they attach to the murder of a few Chinese, that, notwithstanding the efforts of the British Consul, MAIDIN remained at liberty for nearly two years after the commission of the crime.

The execution took place at night. The murderer was bound, with his hands behind his back, in a large canoe, and a noose of rope was placed round his neck. Two men stood behind him; a short stick was inserted in the noose and twisted round and round by the two executioners, thereby causing the rope to compress the windpipe. MAIDIN'S struggles were soon over.

In the case of common people the *kris* is used, the executioner standing behind the criminal and pressing the *kris* downwards, through the shoulder, into the heart. This mode of execution has been retained by the European rulers of Sarawak. In British North Borneo the English mode by hanging has been adopted.

Formerly, when ancient customs were more strictly observed, any person using insulting expressions in talking of members of the Royal family was punished by having his tongue slit, and I was once shewn by the Temenggong, in whose official keeping it was, the somewhat cumbrous pair of scissors wherewith this punishment was inflicted, but I have never heard of its having been used during the last twenty years, although opportunities could not have been wanting.

I was once horrified by being informed by an observant British Naval Officer, who had been to Brunai on duty, that he had been disgusted by noticing, notwithstanding our long connection with Brunai and supposed influence with the Sultan, so barbarous a mode of execution as that of keeping the criminal exposed, without food, day and night, on a stage on high posts in the river. I had never heard of this process, and soon discovered that my friend had mistaken men fishing, for criminals undergoing execution. Two men perch themselves up on posts, some distance apart, and let down by ropes a net into the river. Waiting patiently—and Brunais can sit still contentedly doing nothing for hours—they remain motionless until a shoal of fish passes over the net, when it is partially raised and the fish taken out by a third man, and the operation repeated.

I do not think my naval friend ever published his Brunai reminiscences.

I have already said there is no police force in Brunai; an official makes use of his own slaves to carry out his orders, where an European would call in the police. Neither is there any army and navy, but the theory is that the Sultan and Ministers can call on the Brunai people to follow them to war, but as they give neither pay nor sufficient food their call is not numerously responded to.

Every Brunai man has his own arms, spear, kris and buckler, supplemented by an old English "Tower" musket, or rifle, or by one of Chinese manufacture with an imitation of the Tower mark. The *parang,* or chopper, or cutlass, is always carried by a Malay, being used for all kinds of work, agricultural and other, and is also a useful weapon of offence or defence.

Brunai is celebrated for its brass cannon foundries and still produces handsome pieces of considerable size. PIGAFETTA describes cannon as being frequently discharged at Brunai during his visit there in 1521. Brass guns were formerly part of the currency in Brunai and, even now, you often hear the price of an article given as so many pikuls (a pikul=

133¼lbs), or catties (a catty=1⅓lbs) of brass gun. The brass for the guns is chiefly furnished by the Chinese cash, which is current in the town.

In former days, in addition to brass guns, pieces of grey shirting *(belachu)* and of Nankin *(kain asap)* and small bits of iron were legal tender, and I have seen a specimen of a Brunei copper coinage one Sultan tried to introduce, but it was found to be so easily imitated by his subjects that it was withdrawn from circulation. At the present day silver dollars, Straits Settlements small silver pieces, and the copper coinage of Singapore, Sarawak and British North Borneo all pass current, the copper, however, unfortunately predominating. Recently the Sultan obtained $10,000 of a copper coin of his own from Birmingham, but the traders and the Governments of Singapore and Labuan appear to have discountenanced its use, and he probably will not try a second shipment.

The profit on the circulation of copper coinage, which is only a token, is of course considerable, and the British North Borneo Company obtained a substantial addition to its revenue from the large amount of its coin circulated in Brunai. When the Sultan first mooted the idea of obtaining his own coin from England, one of the Company's officers expostulated feelingly with him, and I was told by an onlooker that the contrast of the expressions of the countenances of the immobile Malay and of the mobile European was most amusing. All that the Sultan replied to the objections of the officer was "It does not signify, Sir, my coin can circulate in your country and yours can circulate in mine," knowing well all the time the profit the Company was making.

The inhabitants of the city of Brunai are very lightly taxed, and there is no direct taxation. As above explained, there is no land tax, nor ground rent, and every man builds his own house and is his own landlord. The right of retailing the following articles is "farmed" out to the highest bidder by the Government, and their price consequently enhanced to the consumer:—Opium (but only a few of the nobles use the drug), foreign tobacco, curry stuff, wines and spirits (not used by the natives), salt, gambier (used for chewing with the betel or *areca* nut), tea (little used by the natives) and earth-nut and coco-nut oil. There are no Municipal rates and taxes, the tidal river acting as a self cleansing street and sewer at the same time; neither are there any demands from a Poor Law Board.

On the other hand, there being no Army, Navy, Police, nor public buildings to keep up, the expenses of Government are wonderfully light also.

Other Government receipts, in addition to the above, are rent of Chinese house-boats or rather shop-boats, pawn-broking and gambling licenses, a "farm" of the export of hides, royalties on sago and gutta percha, tonnage dues on European vessels visiting the port, and others. The salaries and expenses of the Government Departments are defrayed from the revenues of the rivers, or districts attached to them.

Considerable annual payments are now made by Sarawak and British North Borneo for the territorial cessions obtained by them. The annual contribution by Sarawak is about $16,000, and by the British North Borneo $11,800. These sums are apportioned amongst the Sultan and nobles who had interests in the ceded districts. I may say here that the payment by British North Borneo to the Sultan of the State, under the arrangement made by Mr. DENT already referred to, is one of $5,000 per annum.

An annual payment is also made by Mr. W. C. COWIE for the sole right* of working coal in the Sultanate, which he holds for a period of several years. Coal occurs throughout the island of Borneo, and its existence has long been known. It is worked on a small scale in Sarawak and in some portions of Dutch Borneo, and the unsuccessful attempts to develope the coal resources of the Colony of Labuan will be referred to later on.

In the Brunai Sultanate, with which we are at present concerned, coal occurs abundantly in the Brunai river and elsewhere, but it is only at present worked by Mr. COWIE and his partners at Muara, at the mouth of the Brunai river—

---

* This right was transferred by Mr. COWIE to Rája BROOKE in 1833.

Muara, indeed, signifying in Malay a river's mouth. The Revd. J. E. TENNISON-WOOD, well known in Australia as an authority on geological questions, thus describes the Muara coalfields:—"About twenty miles to the South-west of Labuan is the mouth of the Brunai river. Here the rocks are of quite a different character, and much older. There are sandstones, shales, and grits, with ferruginous joints. The beds are inclined at angles of 25 to 45 degrees. They are often altered into a kind of chert. At Muara there is an outcrop of coal seams twenty, twenty-five and twenty-six feet thick. The coal is of excellent quality, quite bitumenised, and not brittle. The beds are being worked by private enterprise. I saw no fossils, but the beds and the coal reminded me much of the older Australian coals along the Hunter river. The mines are of great value. They are rented for a few thousand dollars by two enterprising Scotchmen, from the Sultan of Brunai. The same sovereign would part with the place altogether for little or nothing. Why not have our coaling station there? Or what if Germany, France or Russia should purchase the same from the independent Sultan of Bruñai?" As if to give point to the concluding remarks, a Russian man-of-war visited Muara and Brunai early in 1887, and shewed considerable interest in the coal mines. *

CHAPTER III.

The fairest way, perhaps, of giving my readers an idea of what Brunai was and what it is, will be by quoting first from the description of the Italian PIGAFETTA, who was there in 1521, and then from that of my friend the late Mr. STAIR ELPHIN-STONE DALRYMPLE, who visited the city with me in 1884. PIGAFETTA'S description I extract from CRAWFORD'S *Descriptive Dictionary of the Indian Islands.*

"When," says he, "we reached the city, we had to wait two hours in the *prahu* (boat or barge) until there had arrived two elephants, caparisoned in silk-cloth, and twelve men, each

---

* The British Protectorate has obviated the danger.

furnished with a porcelain vase, covered with silk, to receive and to cover our presents. We mounted the elephants, the twelve men going before, carrying the presents. We thus proceeded to the house of the Governor, who gave us a supper of many dishes. Next day we were left at our leisure until twelve o'clock, when we proceeded to the King's palace. We were mounted, as before, on elephants, the men bearing the gifts going before us. From the Governor's house to the palace the streets were full of people armed with swords, lances and targets; the King had so ordered it. Still mounted on the elephants we entered the court of the palace. We then dismounted, ascended a stair, accompanied by the Governor and some chiefs and entered a great hall full of courtiers. Here we were seated on carpets, the presents being placed near to us. At the end of the great hall, but raised above it, there was one of less extent hung with silken cloth, in which were two curtains, on raising which, there appeared two windows, which lighted the hall. Here, as a guard to the King, there were three hundred men with naked rapiers in hand resting on their thighs. At the farther end of this smaller hall, there was a great window with a brocade curtain before it, on raising which, we saw the King seated at a table masticating betel, and a little boy, his son, beside him. Behind him women only were to be seen. A chieftain then informed us, that we must not address the King directly, but that if we had anything to say, we must say it to him, and he would communicate it to a courtier of higher rank than himself within the lesser hall. This person, in his turn, would explain our wishes to the Governor's brother, and he, speaking through a tube in an aperture of the wall would communicate our sentiments to a courtier near the King, who would make them known to his Majesty. Meanwhile, we were instructed to make three obeisances to the King with the joined hands over the head, and raising, first one foot and then the other, and then kissing the hands. This is the royal salutation.   *   *   * All the persons present in the palace had their loins covered with gold embroidered cloth and silk, wore poiniards with golden hilts, ornamented with pearls and precious stones, and had many rings on their fingers.

* * * * * *

We remounted the elephants and returned to the house of the Governor. * * * After this there came to the house of the Governor ten men, with as many large wooden trays, in each of which were ten or twelve porcelain saucers with the flesh of various animals, that is, of calves, capons, pullets, pea-fowls and others, and various kinds of fish, so that of meat alone there were thirty or two-and-thirty dishes. We supped on the ground on mats of palm-leaf. At each mouthful we drank a porcelain cupful, the size of an egg, of a distilled liquor made from rice. We ate also rice and sweetmeats, using spoons of gold, shaped like our own. In the place where we passed the two nights, there were always burning two torches of white wax, placed on tall chandeliers of silver, and two oil lamps of four wicks each, while two men watched to look after them. Next morning we came on the same elephants to the sea side, where forthwith there were ready for us two *prahus*, in which we were reconducted to the ships." Of the town itself he says :—" The city is entirely built in the salt water, the King's house and those of some chieftains excepted. It contains 25,000 *fires*, or families. The houses are all of wood and stand on strong piles to keep them high from the ground. When the flood tide makes, the women, in boats, go through the city selling necessaries. In front of the King's palace there is a rampart constructed of large bricks, with barbacans in the manner of a fortress, on which are mounted fifty-six brass and six iron cannon." With the exception of the statement concerning the number of families, Mr. CRAWFORD considers PIGAFETTA'S account contains abundant internal evidence of intelligence and truthfulness. I may be allowed to point out that, seeing only the King's house and those of some of the nobles were on *terra firma,* there could have been little use for elephants in the city and probably the two elephants PIGAFETTA mentions were the only ones there, kept for State purposes. It is a curious fact that though in its fauna Borneo much resembles Sumatra, yet, while elephants abound in the latter island, none are to be found in Borneo, except in a restricted area on the North-East Coast, in the territories of the North Borneo Company. It would appear, too, that the tenets of the Mahomedan religion were not strictly observed in those days. Now, no Brunai noble would think of offering you spirits, nor would ladies on any account be permitted to appear in public, especially if Europeans were among the audience. The consumption of spirits seems to have been on a very liberal scale, and it is not surprising to find PIGAFETTA remarking further on that some of the Spaniards became intoxicated. Spoons, whether of gold or other material, have long since been discarded by all respectable Brunais, only Pagans make use of such things, the Mahomedans employ the fingers which Allah has given them. The description of the women holding their market in boats stands good of to-day, but the wooden houses, instead of being on "strong piles," now stand on ricketty, round *nibong* palm posts. The description of the obeisance to the King is scarcely exaggerated, except that it is now performed squatting cross-legged—*sila*—the respectful attitude indoors, from the Sanskrit çîl, to meditate, to worship (for an inferior never stands in the presence of his superior), and has been dispensed with in the case of Europeans, who shake hands. Though the nobles have now comparatively little power, they address each other and are addressed by the commonalty in the most respectful tone, words derived from the Sanskrit being often employed in addressing superiors, or equals if both are of high rank, such as *Baginda, Duli Paduka, Ianda,* and in addressing a superior the speaker only alludes to himself as a slave, *Amba, Sahaya.* I have already referred to the prohibition of the use of yellow by others than the Royal family, and may add that it is a grave offence for a person of ordinary rank to pass the palace steps with his umbrella up, and it is forbidden to him to sit in the after part of his boat or canoe, that place being reserved for nobles. At an audience with the Sultan, or with one of the Wazirs, considerable ceremony is still observed. Whatever the time of the day, a thick bees' wax candle, about three

feet long is lighted and placed on the floor alongside the
European visitor, if he is a person of any rank, and it is
etiquette for him to carry the candle away with him at the
conclusion of his visit, especially if at night. It was a severe
test of the courteous decorum of the Malay nobles when on
one occasion, a young officer, who accompanied me, not only
spilt his cup of coffee over his bright new uniform, but, when
impressively bidding adieu to H. H. the Sultan, stood for
some time unconsciously astride over my lighted candle. Not
a muscle of the faces of the nobles moved, but the Europeans
were scarcely so successful in maintaining their gravity.

Mr. DALRYMPLE'S description of Brunai, furnished to the
Field in August, 1884, is as follows:—"On a broad river,
sweeping round in an imposing curve from the South-East-
ward, with abrupt ranges of sandstone hills, for the most part
cleared of forest, hemming it in on either side, and a glimpse
of lofty blue mountains towering skywards far away to the
North-East, is a long straggling collection of *atap* (thatch
made of leaves of *nibong* palm) and *kajang* (mats of ditto)
houses, or rather huts, built on piles over the water, and
forming a gigantic crescent on either bank of the broad, curv-
ing stream. This is the city of Brunai, the capital of the
Yang di Pertuan, the Sultan of Brunai, *ætat* one hundred or
more, and now in his dotage: the abode of some 15,000
Malays, whose language is as different from the Singapore
Malay as Cornish is from Cockney English, and the coign of
vantage from which a set of effete and corrupt *Pangerans*
extended oppressive rule over the coasts of North-West
Borneo, from Sampanmangiu Point to the Sarawak River in
days gone by, ere British enterprise stepped in, swept the
Sulu and Illanun pirates from the sea, and opened the rivers
to commercial enterprise.

Standing on the summit of one of the above-mentioned hills,
a fine bird's eye view is obtained of the city below. The
ramshackle houses are all built in irregular blocks or clusters,
but present on either side a regular frontage to the broad
river, and following its sweeping curve, form two imposing
crescent, divided by a fine water-way. Behind these main

crescents are various other blocks and clusters of buildings, built higgledy piggledy and without plan of any sort. On the true left bank are some Chinese shops built of brick, and on the opposite bank a brick house of superior pretensions and a waving banner proclaiming the abode of the Chinese Consular Agent of the British North Borneo Company. * * *

A heterogeneous collection of buildings on the right side of the upper part of the city forms the *palace* (save the mark!) of the Sultan himself. A little further down a large, straggling, but substantial plank building, with a corrugated iron roof, marks the abode of the Pangeran Temenggong, a son of the former Sultan and the heir apparent to the throne of Brunai. Two steam launches are lying opposite at anchor, one the property of the Sultan, the other belonging to the heir apparent. * * * * *

"The public reception room of the Sultan's palace is a long apartment with wooden pillars running along either side, and supporting a raised roof. Beyond these on either side, are lateral compartments. At the far end, in the centre of a kind of alcove, is the Sultan's throne. The floors are covered with matting. * * * * *

Although the glories of Brunai have departed, and it is only the shadow of what it was when PIGAFETTA visited it, a certain amount of state is still kept up on occasions. A boat comes sweeping down the river crowded with Malays, a white flag waving from its stern, seven paddles flashing on either side, and an array of white umbrellas midships. *It is* the Pangeran di Gadong coming in state to pay a ceremonial visit. As it sweeps alongside, the Pangeran is seen sitting on a gorgeous carpet, surrounded by his officials. One holds an umbrella over his head, while another holds aloft the *tongkat kraidan,* a long guilded staff, surmounted by a plume of yellow horse hair, which hangs down round it. The most striking point in the attire of the Pangeran and his Officers is the beauty of the *krises* with which they are armed, the handles being of carved ivory ornamented with gold, and the sheaths of beautifully polished wood, resembling satin wood. Cigars and coffee are produced, and a *bichara* ensues. A

Quakers' meeting is no bad metaphor to describe a Malay *bichara*. The Pangerans sit round in a circle smoking solemnly for some time, until a question is put to them, to which a brief reply is given, followed by another prolonged pause.

In this way the business on which they have come is gradually approached.

Their manners are as polished as their faces are immobile, and the way to a Malay's heart lies through his pocket.

To the outsider, Brunai is a city of hideous old women, for such alone are met with in the thronged market place where some hundreds of market boats jostle each other, while their inmates shriek and haggle over their bargains, or during a water promenade while threading the labyrinths of this Oriental Venice; but if acquainted with its intricacies, or if paying a ceremonial visit to any of the leading Pangerans, many a glimpse may be had of some fair skinned beauty peeping through some handy crevice in the *kajang* wall, or, in the latter case, a crowd of light-skinned, dark-eyed houris may be seen looking with all their might out of a window in the harem behind, from which they are privileged to peep into the hall of audience.

The present population of Brunai cannot exceed 12,000 to 15,000 souls, a great number having succumbed to the terrible epidemic of cholera a year ago. The exports consist of sago, gutta percha, camphor, india-rubber, edible birds' nests, gum dammar, etc., and what money there is in the city is almost entirely in the hands of the Chinese traders. * * *

In the old days, when it enjoyed a numerous Chinese population, the surrounding hills were covered with pepper plantations, and there was a large junk trade with China. At present Brunai lives on her exports of jungle produce and sago, furnished by a noble river—the Limbang, whose valley lies but a short distance to the Eastward. One great advantage the city enjoys is a copious supply of pure water, drawn from springs at the base of the hills below the town on the left bank of the river. * * * *

"Such is a slight sketch of Brunai of the Brunais. If the Pangerans are corrupt, the lower classes are not, but are law-abiding, though not industrious. And the day may yet come when their city may lift her head up again, and be to North Borneo what Singapore is to the straits of Malacca."

This description gives a capital idea of modern Brunai, and I would only observe that, from the colour of his flag and umbrellas the nobleman who paid the state visit must have been the Bandahara and not the Di Gadong.

The aged Sultan to whom Mr. DALRYMPLE refers was the late Sultan MUMIM, who, though not in the direct line, was raised to the throne, on the death of the Sultan OMAR ALI SAIFUDIN, to whom he had been Prime Minister, by the influence of the English, towards whom he had always acted as a loyal friend. He was popularly supposed to be over a hundred years old when he died and, though said to have had some fifty wives and concubines, he was childless. He died on the 29th May, 1885, having previously, on the advice of Sir C. C. LEES, then British Consul-General, declared his Temenggong, the son of OMAR ALI SAIFUDIN to be his successor. The Temenggong accended the throne, without any opposition, with the title of Sultan, but found a kingdom distracted by rebellion in the provinces and reduced to less than a fourth of its size when the treaty was made with Great Britain in 1847.

I have said that there is no ground rent in Borneo, and that every one builds his own house and is his own landlord, but I should add that he builds his house in the *kampong,* or parish, to which, according to his occupation, he belongs and into which the city is divided. For instance, on entering the city, the first *kampong* on the left is an important one in a town where fish is the principal article of animal food. It is the *kampong* of the men who catch fish by means of bambu fishing stakes, or traps, described hereafter, and supply the largest quantity of that article to the market; it is known as the *Kampong Pablat.*

Next to it is the *Kampong Perambat,* from the casting net which its inhabitants use in fishing. Another parish is called *Membakut* and its houses are built on firm ground, being principally the shops of Chinese and Klings. The last *kam-*

pong on this side is that of *Burong Pingé,* formerly a very important one, where dwelt the principal and richest Malay traders. It is now much reduced in size, European steamers and Chinese enterprise having altered entirely the character of the trade from the time when the old Brunai *nakodahs* (master or owner of a trading boat) would cruise leisurely up and down the coast, waiting for months at a time in a river while trade was being brought in. The workers in brass, the jewellers, the makers of gold brocade, of mats, of brass guns, the oil manufacturers, and the rice cleaners, all have their own *kampongs,* and are jealous of the honour of each member of their corporation. The Sultan and nearly all the chief nobles have their houses on the true left bank of the river, *i.e.*, on the right bank ascending.

The fishing interest is an important one, and various methods are employed to capture the supply for the market.

The *kélong* is a weir composed of nets made of split bambu, fastened in an upright position, side by side, to posts fixed into the bed of the stream, or into the sand in the shallow water of a harbour. There are two long rows of these posts with attached nets, one much longer than the other which gradually converge in the deeper water, where a simple trap is constructed with a narrow entrance. The fish passing up or down stream, meeting with the obstruction, follow up the walls of the *kélong* and eventually enter the trap, whence they are removed at low water. These *kélong,* or fishing stakes as they are termed, are a well known sight to all travellers entering Malay ports and rivers. All sorts of fish are caught in this way, and alligators of some size are occasionally secured in them.

The *rambat* is a circular casting net, loaded with leaden or iron weights at the circumference, and with a spread sometimes of thirty feet. Great skill, acquired by long practice, is shewn by the fisherman in throwing this net over a shoal of fish which he has sighted, in such a manner that all the outer edge touches the water simultaneously; the weights then cause the edges of the circumference to sink and gradually close together, encompassing the fish, and the net is drawn up by a rope attached to its centre, the other end of which the fisherman had retained in his hand. The skill of the thrower is further enhanced by the fact that he, as a rule, balances himself in the bow of a small "dug-out," or canoe, in which a European could scarcely keep his footing at all. The *rambat* can also be thrown from the bank, or the beach, and is used in fresh and salt water. Only small fish and prawns are caught in this way. Prawns are also caught in small *kélongs* with very fine split bambu nets, but a method is also employed in the Brunai river which I have not heard of elsewhere. A specially prepared canoe is made use of, the gunwale on one side being cut away and its place taken up by a flat ledge, projecting over the water. The fisherman sits paddling in the stern, keeping the ledged side towards the bank and leaning over so as to cause the said ledge to be almost level with the water.

From the same side there projects a long bambu, with wooden teeth on its under side, like a comb, fastened to the stern, but projecting outwards, forwards and slightly upwards, the teeth increasing in length towards its far end, and as they sweep the surface of the water the startled prawns, shut in by the bank on one side, in their efforts to avoid the teeth of the comb, jump into the canoe in large quantities.

I have described the method of using the dip net, or *scrambau*, on page 30. Many kinds of nets are in use, one—the *pukat*—being similar to our seine or drag net.

The hook and line are also used, especially for deep sea fishing, and fish of large size are thus caught.

A favourite occasional amusement is *tuba* fishing. The *tuba* is a plant the juice of which has strong narcotic properties. Bundles of the roots are collected and put into the bottom of the canoes, and when the fishing ground is reached, generally a bend in a river, or the mouth of a stream which is barred at low tide, water is poured over the *tuba* and the juice expressed by beating it with short sticks. The fluid, thus charged with the narcotic poison, is then baled out of the canoes into the stream and the surface is quickly covered by all sorts of fish in all stages of intoxication, the smaller ones even succumbing altogether to the poison.

The large fish are secured by spearing, amid much excitement, the eager sportsmen often overbalancing themselves and falling headlong into the water to the great amusement of the more lucky ones. I remember reading an account of a dignified representative of Her Majesty once joining in the sport and displaying a pair of heels in this way to his admiring subjects. The *tuba* does not affect the flesh of the fish, which is brought to the table without any special preparation.

The principal export from Brunai is sago flour. The sago palm is known to the natives under the name of *rumbiah*, the pith, after its first preliminary washing, is called *lamantah* (*i.e.*, raw), and after its preparation for export by the Chinese, *sagu*. The botanical name is *Metroxylon*, *M. Lævis* being that of the variety the trunk of which is unprotected, and *M. Rumphii* that of the kind which is armed with long and strong spikes, serving to ward off the attacks of the wild pigs from the young palm.

This palm is indigenous in the Malayan Archipelago and grows to the height of twenty to forty feet, in swampy land along the banks of rivers not far from the sea, but out of the reach of tidal influences. A plantation once started goes "on for ever," with scarcely any care or attention from the proprietor, as the palm propagates itself by numerous off-shots, which take the place of the parent tree when it is cut down for the purpose of being converted into food, or when it dies, which, unlike most other palms, it does after it has once flowered and seeded, *i.e.*, after it has attained the age of ten or fifteen years.

It can also be propagated from the seed, but these are often unproductive.

If required for food purposes, the sago palm must be cut down at its base before it begins to flower, as afterwards the pith or *farina* becomes dried up and useless. The trunk is then stripped of its leaves and, if it is intended to work it up at its owner's house, it is cut into convenient lengths and floated down the river; if the pith is to be extracted on the spot the trunk is split in two, longitudinally, and is found to contain a mass of starchy pith, kept together by filaments of woody fibre, and when this is worked out by means of bambu hatchets nothing but a thin rind, the outer bark, is left. To separate the starch from the woody fibre, the pith is placed on a mat in a frame work over a trough by the river side; the sago washer then mounts up and, pouring fresh water over the pith, commences vigorously dancing about on it with his bare feet, the result being that the starch becomes dissolved in the water and runs off with it into the trough below, while the woody fibre remains on the mat and is thrown away, or, if the washer is not a Mahomedan, used for fatening pigs. The starch thus obtained is not yet quite pure, and under the name of *lamantah* is sold to Chinese and undergoes a further process of washing, this time by hand, in large, solid, wooden troughs and tubs. When sufficiently purified, it is sun-dried and, as a fine white flour, is packed in gunny bags for the Singapore market. At Singapore, some of this flour—a very small proportion—is converted into the pearl sago of the shops, but the greater portion is sent on direct to Europe, where it is used for sizing cloth, in the manufacture of beer, for confectionery, &c.

It will be seen that the sago palm thus affords food and also employment to a considerable number of both natives and Chinese and, requiring little or no trouble in cultivation, it is a perfect gift of the gods to the natives in the districts where it occurs. It is a curious fact that, though abounding in Sarawak, in the districts near Brunai and in the southern parts of British North Borneo on the West Coast, it seems to stop short suddenly at the Putatan River, near Gaya Bay, and is not found indigenous in the North nor on the North-East. Some time ago I sent a quantity of young shoots to a Chief living on the Labuk River, near Sandakan, on the East Coast, but have not yet heard whether they have proved a success.

A nasty sour smell is inseparable from a sago factory, but the health of the coolies, who live in the factory, does not appear to be affected by it.

The Brunais and natives of sago districts consume a considerable quantity of sago flour, which is boiled into a thick, tasteless paste, called *boyat* and eaten by being twisted into a large ball round a stick and inserted into the mouth—an ungraceful operation. Tamarind, or some very acid sauce is used to impart to it some flavour. Sago is of course cheaper than rice, but the latter is, as a rule, much preferred by the native, and is found more nutritious and *lasting*. LOGAN, in the *Journal of the Indian Archipelago,* calculates that three sago palms yield more nutritive matter than an acre of wheat, and six trees more than an acre of potatoes. The plantain and banana also flourish, under cultivation, in Borneo, and Mr. BURBIDGE, in his preface to the *Gardens of the Sun,* points out that it fruits all the year round and that its produce is to that of wheat as 133 : 1, and to that of the potato as 44 : 1. What a Paradise! some of my readers will exclaim. There can be no want here! I am sure the figures and calculations above quoted are absolutely correct, but I have certainly seen want and poverty in Borneo, and these tropical countries are not quite the earthly paradises which some old writers would have us believe. For our poor British "unemployed," at any rate, I fear Borneo can never be a refuge, as the sun would there be more fatal than the deadly cold here, and the race could not be kept up without visits to colder climates. But if sago and bananas are so plentiful and so nourishing, as we are taught by the experts, it does seem somewhat remarkable, in this age of invention, that some means cannot be devised of bringing together the prolific food stores of the East and the starving thousands of the West.

Both before, during and after the day's work, the Malays, man and woman, boy and girl, solace and refresh themselves with tobacco and with the areca-nut, or the *betel* nut as, for some unexplained reason, it is called in English books, though *betel* is the name of the pepper leaf in which the areca-nut is wrapped and with which it is masticated.

A good deal of the tobacco now used in Brunai is imported from Java or Palembang (Sumatra), but a considerable portion is grown in the hilly districts on the West Coast of North Borneo, in the vicinity of Gaya Bay, by the Muruts. It is unfermented and sun-dried, but has not at all a bad flavour

and is sometimes used by European pipe smokers. The
Brunai Malays and the natives generally, as a rule, smoke the
tobacco in the form of cigarettes, the place of paper being
taken by the fine inner leaf of the *nipa* palm, properly prepared by drying. The Court cigarettes are monstrous things,
fully eight inches long sometimes, and deftly fashioned by the
fingers of the ladies of the harem.

Some of the inland natives, who are unable to procure *nipa*
leaf *(dahun kirei)*, use roughly made wooden pipes, and the
leaf of the maize plant is also occasionally substituted for the
nipa. It is a common practice with persons of both sexes to
insert a "quid" of tobacco in their cheek, or between the
upper lip and the gum. This latter practice does not add to
the appearance of a race not overburdened with facial charms.
The tobacco is allowed to remain in position for a long time,
but it is not chewed. The custom of areca-nut chewing has
been so often described that I will only remind the reader
that the nut is the produce of a graceful and slender palm,
which flourishes under cultivation in all Malayan countries
and is called by Malays *pinang*. It is of about the size of a
nutmeg and, for chewing, is cut into pieces of convenient size
and made into a neat little packet with the green leaf of the
aromatic betel pepper plant, and with the addition of a little
gambier (the inspissated juice of the leaves of the *uncaria
gambir*) and of fine lime, prepared by burning sea shells.
Thus prepared, the bolus has an undoubtedly stimulating
effect on the nerves and promotes the flow of saliva. I have
known fresh vigour put into an almost utterly exhausted boat's
crew by their partaking of this stimulant.

It tinges the saliva and the lips bright red, but, contrary to
a very commonly received opinion, has no effect of making
the teeth black. This blackening of the teeth is produced by
rubbing in burnt coco-nut shell, pounded up with oil, the
dental enamel being sometimes first filed off. Toothache and
decayed teeth are almost unknown amongst the natives, but
whether this is in some measure due to the chewing of the
areca-nut I am unable to say.

It used to be a disagreeable, but not unusual sight, to see

the old Sultan at an audience remove the areca-nut he had been masticating and hand it to a small boy, who placed it in his mouth and kept it there until the aged monarch again required it.

The clothing of the Brunai Malays is simple and suitable to the climate. The one garment common to men, women and children is the *sarong,* which in its general signification means a sheath or covering, *e.g.,* the sheath of a sword is a *sarong,* and the envelope enclosing a letter is likewise its *sarong.* The *sarong* or sheath of the Brunai human being is a piece of cotton cloth, of Tartan pattern, sewn down the side and resembling an ordinary skirt, or petticoat, except that it is not pleated or attached to a band at the waist and is, therefore, the same width all the way down. It is worn as a petticoat, being fastened at the waist sometimes by a belt or girdle, but more often the upper part is merely twisted into its own folds. Both men and women frequently wear nothing but this garment, the men being naked from the waist up, but the women generally concealing the breasts by fastening the *sarong* high up under the arms ; but for full dress the women wear in addition a short sleeved jacket of dark blue cotton cloth, reaching to the waist, the tight sleeves being ornamented with a row of half-a-dozen jingling buttons, of gold if possible, and a round hat of plaited *pandan* (screw-pine) leaves, or of *nipa* leaf completes the Brunai woman's costume. No stockings, slippers, or shoes are worn. Ladies of rank and wealth substitute silk and gold brocade for the cotton material used by their poorer sisters and, in lieu of a hat, cover their head and the greater part of the face with a *selendang,* or long scarf of gold brocade. They occasionally also wear slippers. The gold brocade is a specialty of Brunai manufacture and is very handsome, the gold thread being woven in tasteful patterns on a ground of yellow, green, red or dark blue silk. The materials are obtained from China. The cotton *sarongs* are also woven in Brunai of European cotton twist, but inferior and cheap imitations are now imported from Switzerland and Manchester. In addition to the *sarong,* the Brunai man, when fully dressed, wears a pair of loose cotton trowsers, tied round the waist, and in this case the *sarong* is so folded as to reach only half way down to the knee, instead of to the ankle, as ordinarily.

A short sleeved cotton jacket, generally white, covers his body and his head dress is a small coloured kerchief called *dastar*, the Persian word for turban.

The nobles wear silks instead of cottons and with them a small but handsome *kris*, stuck into the *sarong*, is *de rigueur* for full dress. A gold or silver betel-nut box might almost be considered as part of the full dress, as they are never without one on state occasions, it being carried by an attendant.

The women are fond of jewellery, and there are some clever gold and silversmiths in the city, whose designs appear to be imitated from the Javanese. Rings, earrings, broaches to fasten the jacket at the neck, elaborate hairpins, massive silver or gold belts, with large gold buckles, and bracelets of gold or silver are the usual articles possessed by a lady of position.

The characteristic earring is quite a specialty of Brunai art, and is of the size and nearly the shape of a very large champagne cork, necessitating a huge hole being made for its reception in the lobes of the ear. It is made hollow, of gold or silver, or of light wood gilt, or sometimes only painted, or even quite plain, and is stuck, lengthwise, through the hole in the ear, the ends projecting on either side. When the ladies are not in full dress, this hole occasionally affords a convenient receptacle for the cigarette, or any other small article not in use for the time being.

The men never wear any jewellery, except, perhaps, one silver ring, which is supposed to have come from the holy city—Mecca.

The Malay *kris* is too well known to need description here. It is a dagger or poignard with a blade varying in length from six inches to two feet. This blade is not invariably wavy, or serpentine, as often supposed, but is sometimes quite straight. It is always sharp on both edges and is fashioned from iron imported from Singapore, by Brunai artificers. Great taste is displayed in the handle, which is often of delicately carved ivory and gold, and just below the attachment of the handle, the blade is broadened out, forming a hilt, the under edge of which is generally fancifully carved. Age adds greatly to the value of the *kris* and the history of many is handed down. The highest price I know of being given for a Brunai *kris* was $100, paid by the present Sultan for one he presented to the British North Borneo Company on his accession to the throne, but I have heard of higher prices being asked. Very handsomely grained and highly polished wood is used for the sheath and the two pieces forming it are frequently so skilfully joined as to have the appearance of being in one. Though naturally a stabbing weapon, the Malays of Brunai generally use it for cutting, and after an *amok* the blade employed is often found bent out of all shape.

The *parang* is simply an ordinary cutlass, with a blade two feet in length. As we generally carry a pocket knife about with us, so the Brunai Malay always wears his *parang*, or has it near at hand, using it for every purpose where cutting is required, from paring his nails to cutting the posts of which his house is built, or weeding his patch of rice land.

With this and his *bliong* he performs all his carpentry work; from felling the enormous timber tree in the jungle to the construction of his house and boat. The *bliong* is indeed a most useful implement and can perform wonders in the hands of a Malay. It is in the shape of a small adze, but according to the way it is fitted into the handle it can be used either as an axe or adze. The Malays with this instrument can make planks and posts as smooth as a European carpenter is able to do with his plane.

The *parang ilang* is a fighting weapon, with a peculiarity in the shape of the blade which, Dr. TAYLOR informs me, is not known to occur in the weapons of any other country, and consists in the surface of the near side being flat, as in an ordinary blade, while that of the off side is distinctly convex. This necessitates rather careful handling in the case of a novice, as the convexity is liable to cause the blade to glance off any hard substance and inflict a wound on its wielder.

This weapon is manufactured in Brunai, but is the proper arm of the Kyans and, now, also of the Sarawak Dyaks, who are closely allied to them and who, in this as in other matters, such as the curious perforation of a part of their person, which has been described by several writers, are following their example. The Kyans were once the most formidable Sub-Malay tribe in Northern Borneo and have been alluded to in preceding pages. On the West coast, their headquarters is the Baram River, which has recently been added to Sarawak, but they stretch right across to the East Coast and Dutch territory.

There are many kinds of canoes, from the simple dug-out, with scarcely any free-board, to the *pakerangan,* a boat the construction of which is confined to only two rivers in North Borneo. It is built up of planks fastened together by wooden pegs, carvel fashion, on a small keel, or *lunas.* It is sharp at both ends, has very good lines, is a good sea boat and well adapted for crossing river bars. It is not made in Brunai itself, but is bought from the makers up the coast and invariably used by the Brunai fishermen, who are the best and most powerful paddlers to be found anywhere. The trading boats—*prahus* or *tongkangs*—are clumsy, badly fastened craft, not often exceeding 30 tons burthen, and modelled on the Chinese junk, generally two-masted, the foremast raking forward, and furnished with rattan rigging and large lug sails. This forward rake, I believe, was not unusual, in former days, in European craft, and is said to aid in tacking. The natives now, however, are getting into the way of building and rigging their boats in humble imitation of the Europeans. The *prahus* are generally furnished with long sweeps, useful when the wind falls and in ascending winding rivers, when the breeze cannot be depended on. The canoes are propelled and steered by single-bladed paddles. They also generally carry a small sail, often made of the remnants of different gaily coloured garments, and a fleet of little craft with their gaudy sails is a pleasing sight on a fresh, bright morning. At the sports held by the Europeans on New Year's Day, the Queen's Birthday and other festivals, native canoe races are always included and are contested with the keenest possible excitement by the competitors. A Brunai Malay takes to the water and to his tiny canoe almost before he is able to walk. Use has with him become second nature and, really, I have known some Brunai men paddle all day long, chatting and singing and chewing betel-nut, as though they felt it no exertion whatever.

In the larger canoes one sees the first step towards a fixed rudder and tiller, a modified form of paddle being fixed securely to one *side* of the stern, in such a way that the blade can be turned so as either to have its edges fore and aft, or its sides presented at a greater or less angle to the water, according to the direction in which it is desired to steer the boat.

I was much interested, in going over the Pitt-Rivers collection, at the Oxford University Museum, to find that in the model of a Viking boat the steering gear is arranged in almost exactly the same manner as that of the modern Malay canoe; and indeed, the lines generally of the two boats are somewhat alike.

To the European novice, paddling is severe work, more laborious than rowing; but then a Brunai man is always in "training," more or less; he is a teetotaller and very temperate in eating and drinking; indeed the amount of fluid they take is, considering the climate, wonderfully small. They scarcely drink during meals, and afterwards, as a rule, only wash their mouths out, instead of taking a long draught like the European.

Mr. DALRYMPLE is right in saying that a State visit is like a Quakers' meeting. Seldom is any important business more than broached on such an occasion; the details of difficult negotiations are generally discussed and arranged by means of confidential agents, who often find it to their pecuniary advantage to prolong matters to the limit of their employer's patience. The Brunai Malays are very nice, polite fellows to have to deal with, but they have not the slightest conception of the value of time, and the expression *nanti dahulu* (wait a bit) is as often in their mouths as that of *malua* (by-and-by) is by Miss GORDON CUMMING said to be in those of the Fijians.

A lady friend of mine, who found a difficulty in acquiring Malay, pronounced *nanti dahulu,* or *nanti dulu* as generally spoken, "nanty doodle," and suggested that "the nanty doodles" could be a good name for "the Brunai Malays."

As writing is a somewhat rare accomplishment, state documents are not signed but sealed—"*chopped*" it is called—and much importance is accordingly attached to the official seals or *chops,* which are large circular metal stamps, and the *chop* is affixed by oiling the stamps, blacking it over the flame of a candle and pressing it on the document to be sealed. The *chop* bears, in Arabic characters, the name, style and title of the Official using it. The Sultan's Chop is the Great Seal of State and is distinguished by being the only one of which the circumference can be quite round and unbroken; the edges of those of the Wazirs are always notched.

By the aboriginal tribes of Borneo, the Brunai people are always spoken of as *Orang Abai,* or Abai men, but though I have often enquired both of the aborigines and of the Brunais themselves, I have not been able to obtain any explanation of the term, nor of its derivation.

As already stated, the religion of the Brunais is Mahomedanism; but they do not observe its precepts and forms with any very great strictness, nor are they proselytisers, so that comparatively few of the surrounding pagans have embraced the religion of their conquerors.

Many of their old superstitions still influence them, as, in the early days of Christianity, the belief in the old heathen gods and goddesses were found underlying the superstructure of the new faith and tinging its ritual and forms of worship. There still flourishes and survives, influencing to the present day the life of the Brunais, the old Spirit worship and a real belief in the power of evil spirits (*hantus*) to cause ill-luck, sickness and death, to counteract which spells, charms and prayers are made use of, together with propitiatory offerings. Most of them wear some charm to ward off sickness, and others to shield them from death in battle. If you are travelling in the jungle and desire to quench your thirst at a brook, your Brunai follower will first lay his *parang,* or cutlass in the bed of the stream, with its point towards the source, so that the Spirit of the brook shall be powerless to harm you.

In caves and on small islands you frequently find platforms and little models of houses and boats—propitiatory offerings to *hantus*. In times of general sickness a large model of a boat is sometimes made and decked with flags and launched out to sea in the hope that the evil spirit who has brought the epidemic may take his departure therein. At Labuan it was difficult to prevail on a Malay messenger to pass after sunset by the gaol, where executions took place, or by the churchyard, for fear of the ghosts haunting those localities.

Javanese element, and Hindu work in gold has been discovered buried in the island of Pappan, situated between Labuan and Brunai. Mr. INCHE MAHOMET, H. B. M.'s Consular Agent in Brunai, was good enough to procure for me a native history of Brunai, called the *Telselah Besar*, or principal history. This history states that the first Mahomedan Sovereign of Brunai was Sultan MAHOMET and that, before his conversion and invesiture by the Sultan of Johor, his kingdom had been tributary to the State of Majapahit, on the fall of which kingdom the Brunai Government transferred its allegiance to Johor. Majapahit* was the last Javanese kingdom professing Hinduism, and from its overthrow dates the triumph of Mahomedanism in Java. This occurred in A.D. 1478, which, if the chronicle can be trusted, must have been about the period of the commencement of the Mahomedan period in Brunai. Inclusive of this Sultan MAHOMET and of the late Sultan MUMIM, who died in May, 1885, twenty-three Mahomedan Sultans have reigned in Brunai and, allowing eighteen years for an average reign, this brings us within a few years of the date assigned to the overthrow of the kingdom of Majapahit, and bears testimony to the reliability of the chronicle. I will quote the first few paragraphs of the *Telselah*, as they will give the reader an idea of a Brunai history and also because they allude to the connection of the Chinese with Borneo and afford a fanciful explanation of the origin of the name of the mountain of

---

* CRAWFURD'S Dictionary—Indian Islands—*Majapait*.

Kinabalu, in British North Borneo, which is 13,700 feet in height:—" This is the genealogy of all the Rájas who have
" occupied the royal throne of the Government of Brunai, the
" abode of peace, from generation to generation, who inherited
" the royal drum and the bell, the tokens from the country of
" Johore, *kamal almakam,* and who also possessed the royal
" drum from Menangkabau, namely, from the country of Sagun-
" tang.

" This was the commencement of the kingdom of Brunai and
" of the introduction of the Mahomedan religion and of the
" Code of Laws of the prophet, the beloved of God, in the
" country of Brunai—that is to say (in the reign of) His High-
" ness Sultan MAHOMET. But before His Majesty's time the
" country of Brunai was still infidel, and a dependency of
" Majapahit. On the death of the Batara of Majapahit and of
" the PATIH GAJA MEDAH the kingdom of Majapahit fell, and
" Brunai ceased to pay tribute, which used to consist of one
" jar of the juice of the young betel-nut every year.

" In the time of the Sultan BAHTRI of the kingdom of Johor,
" Tuan ALAK BETATAR and PATIH BERBAHI were summoned
" to Johor, and the former was appointed Sultan MAHOMET
" by the Sultan of Johor, who conferred on him the royal
" drum and assigned him five provinces, namely, Kaluka, Seri-
" bas, Sadong, Samarahan and Sarawak. PATIH BERBAI was
" given the title of Bandhara Sri Maharaja. After a stay of
" some little time in Johor, His Highness the Sultan MAHOMET
" returned to Brunai; but His Highness had no male issue and
" only one daughter. At that time also the Emperor of China
" ordered two of his ministers to obtain possession of the pre-
" cious stone of the dragon of the mountain Kinabalu.
" Numbers of Chinese were devoured by the dragon and still
" possession was not obtained of the stone. For this reason
" they gave the mountain the name of Kinabalu *(Kina=*
" Chinese; *balu=widow).*

" The name of one of the Chinese Ministers was ONG
" KANG and of another ONG SUM PING, and the latter had
" recourse to a stratagem. He made a box with glass
" sides and placed a large lighted candle therein, and

"when the dragon went forth to feed, ONG SUM PING
" seized the precious stone and put the lamp in its place and
" the dragon mistook it for the precious stone. Having now
" obtained possession of the precious stone all the junks set
" sail for China, and when they had got a long way off from
" Kinabalu, ONG KANG asked ONG SUM PING for the stone,
" and thereupon a quarrel ensued beetwen them. ONG KANG
" continued to press his demand for the precious stone, and
" ONG SUM PING became out of humour and sullen and refused
" to return to China and made his way back to Brunai. On
" arriving there, he espoused the Princess, the daughter of
" Sultan MAHOMET, and he obtained the title of Sultan
" AHAMAT.

" The Sultan AHAMAT had one daughter, who was remark-
" ably beautiful. It came to pass that a Sheriff named ALLI,
" a descendant of AMIR HASSAN *(one of the grandchildren
" of the prophet)* came from the country of Taif to Brunai.
" Hearing of the fame of the beauty of the Sultan's daughter,
" he became enamoured of her and the Sultan accepted him
" as his son-in-law and the Government of Brunai was hand-
" ed over to him by His Highness and he was styled Sultan
" BERKAT. He enforced the Code of Laws of the beloved
" of God and erected a mosque in Brunai, and, moreover,
" ordered the Chinese population to make a stone fort."

The connection of the Chinese with Brunai was an important event in Borneo history and it was certainly to them that the flourishing condition of the capital when visited by PIGAFETTA in 1521 was due. They were the sole planters of the pepper gardens, the monopoly of the trade in the produce of which the East India Company negotiated for in 1774, when the crop was reported to the Company to have been 4,000 pikuls, equal to about 240 tons, valued on the spot at $17\frac{1}{4}$ Spanish dollars per pikul. The Company's Agent expressly reported that the Chinese were the only pepper planters, that the aborigines did not plant it, and that the produce was disposed of to Chinese junks, which visited the port and which he trusted would, when the exclusive trade in this article was in the hands of the Company, be diverted from Brunai to Balambangan.

The station at this latter island, as already mentioned, was abandoned in 1775, and the English trade with Brunai appears soon afterwards to have come to an end.

From extracts from the Journal of the Batavia Society of Arts and Sciences published in *The British North Borneo Herald* of the 1st October, 1886, the first mention of Brunai in Chinese history appears to be in the year 669, when the King of Polo, which is stated to be another name for Bunlai (corruption of "Brunai"), sent an envoy to Pekin, who came to Court with the envoy of Siam. Again, in the year 1406, another Brunai envoy was appointed, who took with him a tribute of the products of the country, and the chronicle goes on to say that it is reported "that the present " King is a man from Fukien, who followed CHENG HO when " he went to this country and who settled there."

This account was written in 1618 and alludes to the Chinese shipping then frequenting Brunai. It is by some supposed that the northern portion of Borneo was the destination of the unsuccessful expedition which KUBLAI KHAN sent out in the year 1292.

Towards the close of the eighteenth century a Government seems to have arisen in Brunai which knew not ONG SUM PING and, in 1809, Mr. HUNT reported that Chinese junks had ceased visiting Brunai and, owing no doubt to the rapacious and piratical character of the native Government, the pepper gardens were gradually deserted and the Chinese left the country. A few of the natives had, however, acquired the art of pepper cultivation, especially the Dusuns of Pappar, Kimanis and Bundu and when the Colony of Labuan was founded, 1846, there was still a small trade in pepper with those rivers. The Brunai Rájas, however, received their revenues and taxes in this commodity and their exhorbitant demands gradually led to the abandonment of its cultivation.

These rivers have since passed under the Government of the British North Borneo Company, and in Bundu, owing partly to the security now afforded to life and property and partly to the very high price which pepper at present realizes on account of the Dutch blockade of Achin—Achin having been of late years the principal pepper-growing country—the natives are again turning their attention to this article. I may remark here that the people of Bundu claim and shew evidence of Chinese descent, and even set up in their houses the little altar and joss which one is accustomed to see in Chinamen's shops. The Brunai Malays call the Chinese *Orang Kina* and evidence of their connection with Borneo is seen in such names as *Kina-batangan,* a river near Sandakan on the north-east coast, *Kina-balu,* the mountain above referred to, and *Kina-benua,* a district in Labuan. They have also left their mark in the very superior mode of cultivation and irrigation of rice fields on some rivers on the north-west coast as compared with the primitive mode practised in other parts of Northern Borneo. It is now the object of the Governments of Sarawak and of British North Borneo to attract Chinese to their respective countries by all the means in their power. This has, to a considerable extent, been successfully achieved by the present Rája BROOKE, and a large area of his territory is now under pepper cultivation with a very marked influence on the public revenues. This subject will be again alluded to when I come to speak of British North Borneo.

It would appear that Brunai was once or twice attacked by the Spaniards, the last occasion being in 1645.* It has also had the honour in more recent times, of receiving the attentions of a British naval expedition, which was brought about in this wise. Sir JAMES, then Mr. BROOKE, had first visited Sarawak in 1839 and found the district in rebellion against its ruler, a Brunai Rája named MUDA HASSIM, who, being a friend to the English, received Mr. BROOKE with cordiality. Mr. BROOKE returned to Sarawak in the following year and this time assisted MUDA HASSIM to put down the rebellion and finally, on the 24th September, 1841, the Malay Rája

---

* Captain RODNEY MUNDY, R. N., states that in 1846 he captured at Brunai ten large Spanish brass guns, the longest being 14 feet 6 inches, cast in the time of CHARLES III of Spain and the most beautiful specimens of workmanship he had ever seen. CHARLES III reigned between 1759 and 1788.

retired from his position as Governor in favour of the Englishman.

The agreement to so transfer the Government was not signed without the application of a little pressure, for we find the following account of it in Mr. BROOKE'S Journal, edited by Captain RODNEY MUNDY, R. N., in two volumes, and published by JOHN MURRAY in 1848:—" October 1st, 1841. " Events of great importance have occurred during the last " month. I will shortly narrate them. The advent of the " *Royalist* and *Swift* and a second visit from the *Diana* " on her return from Brunei with the shipwrecked crew of the " *Sultana*, strengthened my position, as it gave evidence " that the Singapore authorities were on the alert, and other- " wise did good to my cause by creating an impression amongst " the natives of my power and influence with the Governor of " the Straits Settlements. Now, then, was my time for push- " ing measures to extremity against my subtle enemy the " arch-intriguer MAKOTA." This Chief was a Malay hostile to English interest. " I had previously made several " strong remonstrances, and urged for an answer to a " letter I had addressed to MUDA HASSIM, in which I had " recapitulated in detail the whole particulars of our agree- " ment, concluding by a positive demand either to allow " me to retrace my steps by repayment of the sums which " he had induced me to expend, or to confer upon me the grant " of the Government of the country according to his repeated " promises; and I ended by stating that if he would not do " either one or the other I *must find means to right myself.* " Thus did I, for the first time since my arrival in the land, " present anything in the shape of a menace before the Rája, " my former remonstrances only going so far as to threaten to " take away my own person and vessels from the river." Mr. BROOKE'S demand for an investigation into MAKOTA'S conduct was politely shelved and Mr. BROOKE deemed "the " moment for action had now arrived. My conscience told me " that I was bound no longer to submit to such injustice, and " I was resolved to test the strength of our respective parties. " Repairing on board the yacht, I mustered my people, explain-

"ed my intentions and mode of operation, and having loaded
" the vessel's guns with grape and canister, and brought her
" broadside to bear, I proceeded on shore with a detachment
" fully armed, and taking up a position at the entrance of the
" Rája's palace, demanded and obtained an immediate audience.
" In a few words I pointed out the villany of MAKOTA, his
" tyranny and oppression of all classes, and my determination
" to attack him by force, and drive him from the country. I
" explained to the Rája that several Chiefs and a large body of
" Siniawan Dyaks were ready to assist me, and the only course
" left to prevent bloodshed was immediately to proclaim me
" Governor of the country. This unmistakeable demonstration
" had the desired effect   *   *   *   None
" joined the party of MAKOTA, and his paid followers were not
" more than twenty in number.

" Under the guns of the *Royalist,* and with a small body of
" men to protect me personally, and the great majority of all
" classes with me, it is not surprising that the negotiation pro-
" ceeded rapidly to a favourable issue. The document was
" quickly drawn up, sealed, signed, and delivered; and on the
" 24th of September, 1841, I was declared Rája and Governor
" of Sarawak amidst the roar of cannon, and a general display
" of flags and banners from the shore and boats on the river."

This is a somewhat lengthy quotation, but the language is so graphic and so honest that I need make no apologies for introducing it and, indeed, it is the fairest way of exhibiting Mr. BROOKE'S objects and reasons and is, moreover, interesting as shewing under what circumstances and conditions the first permanent English settlement was formed in Borneo.

Mr. BROOKE concludes his account of his accession to the Government in words that remind us of another unselfish and modest hero—General GORDON. He says:—" Difficulty
" followed upon difficulty; the dread of pecuniary failure, the
" doubt of receiving support or assistance; this and much
" more presents itself to my mind. But I have tied myself to
" the stake. I have heaped faggots around me. I stand
" upon a cask of gunpowder, and if others bring the torch I
" shall not shrink. I feel within me the firm, unchangeable

"conviction of doing right which nothing can shake. I see
"the benefits I am conferring. The oppressed, the wretched,
"the outlawed have found in me their only protector. They
"now hope and trust; and they shall not be disappointed while
"I have life to uphold them. God has so far used me as a
"humble instrument of his hidden Providence; and whatever
"be the result, whatever my fate, I know the example will
"not be thrown away. I know it tends to a good end in His
"own time. He can open a path for me through all difficulties,
"raise me up friends who will share with me in the task,
"awaken the energies of the great and powerful, so that
"they may protect this unhappy people. I trust it may be so:
"but if God wills otherwise; if the time be not yet arrived; if it
"be the Almighty's will that the flickering taper shall be
"extinguished ere it be replaced by a steady beacon, I submit,
"in the firm and humble assurance that His ways are better
"than my ways, and that the term of my life is better in His
"hands than in my own." On the 1st August, 1842, this cession of Sarawak to Mr. BROOKE was confirmed by His Highness Sultan OMAR ALI SAIFUDIN, under the Great Seal. MUDA HASSIM was the uncle of the Sultan, who was a sovereign of weak, vacillating disposition, at one time guided by the advice of his uncle, who was the leader of the "English party," and expressing his desire for the Queen's assistance to put down piracy and disorder and offering, in return, to cede to the British the island of Labuan; at another following his own natural inclinations and siding altogether with the party of disorder, who were resolved to maintain affairs as they were in the "good old times," knowing that when the reign of law and order should be established their day and their power and ability to aggrandize and enrich themselves at the expense of the aborigines and the common people would come to an end. There is no doubt that Mr. BROOKE himself considered it would be for the good of the country that MUDA HASSIM should be raised to the throne and the Sultan certainly entertained a not altogether ill-founded dread that it was intended to depose him in the latter's favour, the more so as a large majority of the Brunai people were known to be in his

interest. In the early part of 1845 MUDA HASSIM appears to have been in favour with the Sultan, and was publicly announced as successor to the throne with the title of *Sultan Muda* (muda=young, the usual Malay title for the heir apparent to the Crown), and the document recognising the appointment of Mr. BROOKE as the Queen's Confidential Agent in Borneo was written in the name of the Sultan and of MUDA HASSIM conjointly, and concludes by saying that the two writers express the hope that through the Queen's assistance they will be enabled to *settle the Government of Borneo*. In April, 1846, however, Mr. BROOKE received the startling intelligence that in the December, or January previous, the Sultan had ordered the murder of his uncle MUDA HASSIM and of several of the Ràja's brothers and nobles of his party, in all some thirteen Ràjas and many of their followers. MUDA HASSIM, finding resistance useless, retreated to his boat and ignited a cask of powder, but the explosion not killing him, he blew his brains out with a pistol. His brother, Pangeran BUDRUDIN, one of the most enlightened nobles in Brunai, likewise terminated his existence by an explosion of gunpowder. Representations being made to Sir THOMAS COCHRANE, the Admiral in command of the station, he proceeded in person to Borneo with a squadron of eight vessels, including two steamers. The Sultan, foreseeing the punishment that was inevitable, erected some well-placed batteries to defend his town. Only the two steamers and one sailing vessel of war, together with boats from the other vessels and a force of six hundred men were able to ascend the river and, such was the rotten state of the kingdom of Borneo Proper and so unwarlike the disposition of its degenerate people that after firing a few shots, whereby two of the British force were killed and a few wounded, the batteries were deserted, the Sultan and his followers fled to the jungle, and the capital remained at the Admiral's disposition. Captain RODNEY MUNDY, accompanied by Mr. BROOKE, with a force of five hundred men was despatched in pursuit of His Highness, but it is needless to add that, though the difficulties of marching through a trackless country under a tropical downpour of rain were pluckily surmounted, it was found impossible to come up with the Royal fugitive. Negotiations were subsequently entered into with the Prime Minister, Pangeran MUMIM, an intelligent noble, who afterwards became Sultan, and on the 19th July, 1846, the batteries were razed to the ground and the Admiral issued a Proclamation to the effect that hostilities would cease if the Sultan would return and govern lawfully, suppress piracy and respect his engagements with the British Government; but that if he persisted in his evil courses the squadron would return and burn down the capital. The same day Admiral COCHRANE and his squadron steamed away. It is perhaps superfluous to add that this was the first and the last time that the Brunai Government attempted to try conclusions with the British, and in the following year a formal treaty was concluded to which reference will be made hereafter.

(To be continued.)

Chapter IV.

Having alluded to the circumstances under which the Government of Sarawak became vested in the BROOKE family, it may be of interest if I give a brief outline of the history of that State under its European rulers up to the present time. The territory acquired by Sir JAMES BROOKE in 1841 and known as Sarawak Proper, was a small district with a coast line of sixty miles and with an average depth inland of fifty miles—an area of three thousand square miles. Since that date, however, rivers and districts lying to the northward have been acquired by cessions for annual payments from the Brunai Government and have been incorporated with the original district of Sarawak, which has given its name to the enlarged territory, and the present area of Raja BROOKE'S possessions is stated to be about 40,000 square miles, supporting a population of 280,000 souls, and possessing a coast line of 380 miles. The most recent acquisition of territory was in 1884, so that the young State has shewn a very vigorous growth since its birth in 1841—at the rate of about 860 square miles a year, or an increase of thirteen times its original size in the space of forty-three years.

Now, alas, there are no "more lands to conquer," or acquire, unless the present kingdom of Brunai, or Borneo Proper, as it is styled by the old geographers, is altogether swallowed up by its offspring, which, under its white ruler, has developed a vitality never evinced under the rule of the Royal house of Brunai in its best days.*

The limit of Sarawak's coast line to the South-West is Cape, or *Tanjong*, Datu, on the other side of which commences the Dutch portion of Borneo, so that expansion in that direction is barred. To the North-East the boundary is Labuk Pulai the Eastern limit of the watershed, on the coast, of the important river Barram which was acquired by Raja BROOKE, in 1881, for an annual payment of £1,000. Beyond this commences what is left of the Brunai Sultanate, there being but one stream of any importance between the Barram river and that on which the capital—Brunai—is situated. But Sarawak does not rest here; it acquired, in 1884, from the then Pangeran Tumonggong, who is now Sultan, the Trusan, a river to the East of the Brunai, under somewhat exceptional circumstances. The natives of the river were in rebellion against the Brunai Government, and in November, 1884, a party of Sarawak Dyaks, who had been trading and collecting jungle produce in the neighbourhood of the capital, having been warned by their own Government to leave the country because of its disturbed condition, and having further been warned also by the Sultan not to enter the Trusan, could not refrain from visiting that river on their homeward journey, in order to collect some outstanding trade debts. They were received is so friendly a manner, that their suspicions were not in the slightest degree aroused, and they took no precautions, believing themselves to be amongst friends. Suddenly in the night they were attacked while asleep in their boats, and the whole party, numbering about seventeen, massacred, with the exception of one man who, though wounded, managed to effect his escape and ultimately found his way to Labuan, where he was treated in the Government Hospital and made a recovery. The heads of the murdered men were, as is customary, taken by the murderers. No very distinct reason can be given for the attack, except that the Trusan

---

* On the 17th March, 1890 the Limbang River was forcibly annexed by Sarawak, subject to the Queen's sanction.

people were in a "slaying" mood, being on the "war-path" and in arms against their own Government, and it has also been said that those particular Dyaks happened to be wearing trowsers instead of their ordinary *chawat*, or loin cloth, and, as their enemies, the Brunais, were trowser-wearers, the Trusan people thought fit to consider all natives wearing such extravagant clothing as their enemies. The Sarawak Government, on hearing of the incident, at once despatched Mr. MAXWELL, the Chief Resident, to demand redress. The Brunai Government, having no longer the warlike Kyans at their beck and call, that tribe having passed to Raja BROOKE with the river Barram, were wholly unable to undertake the punishment of the offenders. Mr. MAXWELL then demanded as compensation the sum of $22,000, basing his calculations on the amount which some time previously the British Government had exacted in the case of some British subjects who had been murdered in another river.

This demand the bankrupt Government of Brunai was equally incompetent to comply with, and, thereupon, the matter was settled by the transfer of the river to Raja BROOKE in consideration of the large annual payment of $4,500, two years' rental—$9,000, being paid in advance, and Sarawak thus acquired, as much by good luck as through good management, a *pied à terre* in the very centre of the Brunai Sultanate and practically blocked the advance of their northern rivals—the Company—on the capital. This river was the *kouripan* (see *ante*, page 26) of the present Sultan, and a feeling of pique which he then entertained against the Government of British North Borneo, on account of their refusing him a monetary loan to which he conceived he had a claim, caused him to make this cession with a better grace and more readily than might otherwise have been the case, for he was well aware that the British North Borneo Company viewed with some jealousy the extension of Sarawak territory in this direction, having, more than probably, themselves an ambition to carry their own southern boundary as near to Brunai as circumstances would admit. The same feeling on the part of the Tumonggong induced him to listen to Mr. MAXWELL'S proposals for the cession to Sarawak of a still more important river—the Limbang—one on which the existence of Brunai itself as an independent State may be said to depend. But the then reigning Sultan and the other Ministers of State refused their sanction, and the Tumonggong, since his accession to the throne, has also very decidedly changed his point of view, and is now in accord with the large majority of his Brunai subjects to whom such a cession would be most distasteful. It should be explained that the Limbang is an important sago-producing river, close to the capital and forming an actual portion of the Brunai river itself, with the waters of which it mingles; indeed, the Brunai river is probably the former mouth of the Limbang, and is itself but a salt-water inlet, producing nothing but fish and prawns. As the Brunais themselves put it, the Limbang is their *priuk nasi*, their rice pot, an expression which gains the greater force when it is remembered that rice is the chief food with this eastern people, in a more emphatic sense even than bread is with us. This question of the Limbang river will afford a good instance and specimen of the oppressive government, or want of government, on the part of the Brunai rulers, and I will return to it again, continuing now my short glance at Sarawak's progress. Raja BROOKE has had little difficulty in establishing his authority in the districts acquired from time to time, for not only were the people glad to be freed from the tyranny of the Brunai Rajas, but the fame of both the present Raja and of his famous uncle Sir JAMES had spread far and wide in Borneo, and, in addition, it was well known that the Sarawak Government had at its back its war-like Dyak tribes, who, now that "head-hunting" has been stopped amongst them, would have heartily welcomed the chance of a little legitimate fighting and "at the commandment of the Magistrate to wear weapons and serve in the wars," as the XXXVIIth Article of our Church permits. In the Trusan, the Sarawak flag was freely distributed and joyfully accepted, and in a short time the Brunai river was dotted with little roughly "dug-out" canoes, manned by repulsive-looking, naked, skin-diseased savages, each proudly flying an enormous Sarawak ensign, with its Christian symbol of the Cross, in the Muhammadan capital.

A fine was imposed and paid for the murder of the Sarawak Dyaks, and the heads delivered up to Mr. A. H. EVERETT, the Resident of the new district, who thus found his little launch on one occasion decorated in an unusual manner with these ghastly trophies, which were, I believe, forwarded to the sorrowing relatives at home.

In addition to these levies of warriors expert in jungle fighting, on which the Government can always count, the Raja has a small standing army known as the "Sarawak Rangers," recruited from excellent material—the natives of the country—under European Officers, armed with breech-loading rifles, and numbering two hundred and fifty or three hundred men. There is, in addition, a small Police Force, likewise composed of natives, as also are the crews of the small steamers and launches which form the Sarawak Navy. With the exception, therefore, of the European Officers, there is no foreign element in the military, naval and civil forces of the State, and the peace of the people is kept by the people themselves, a state of things which makes for the stability and popularity of the Government, besides enabling it to provide for the defence of the country and the preservation of internal order at a lower relative cost than probably any other Asiatic country the Government of which is in the hand of Europeans. Sir JAMES BROOKE did not marry, and died in 1868, having appointed as his successor the present Raja CHARLES JOHNSON, who has taken the name of BROOKE, and has proclaimed his eldest son, a youth of sixteen, heir apparent, with the title of Raja Muda. The form of Government is that of an absolute monarchy, but the Raja is assisted by a Supreme Council composed of two European officials and four natives nominated by himself. There is also a General Council of some fifty members, which is not usually convened more frequently than once in two or three years. For administrative purposes, the country is divided into Divisions, each under a European Resident with European and Native Assistants. The Resident administers justice, and is responsible for the collection of the Revenue and the preservation of order in the district, reporting direct to the Raja. Salaries are on an equitable scale, and the regulations for leave and pension on retirement are conceived in a liberal spirit.

There is no published Code of Laws, but the Raja, when the occasion arises, issues regulations and proclamations for the guidance of officials, who, in criminal cases, follow as much as possible the Indian Criminal Code. Much is left to the common sense of the Judicial Officers, native customs and religious prejudices receive due consideration, and there is a right of appeal to the Raja. Slavery was in full force when Sir JAMES BROOKE assumed the Government, all captives in the numerous tribal wars and piratical expeditions being kept or sold as slaves.

Means were taken to mitigate as much as possible the condition of the slaves, not, as a rule, a very hard one in these countries, and to gradually abolish the system altogether, which latter object was to be accomplished by 1888.

The principal item of revenue is the annual sum paid by the person who secures from the Government the sole right of importing, preparing for consumption, and retailing opium throughout the State. The holder of this monopoly is known as the "Opium Farmer," and the monopoly is termed the "Opium Farm." These expressions have occasionally given rise to the notion that the opium-producing poppy is cultivated locally under Government supervision, and I have seen it included among the list of Borneo products in a recent geographical work. It is evident that the system of farming out this monopoly has a tendency to limit the consumption of the drug, as, owing to the heavy rental paid to the Government, the retail price of the article to the consumer is very much enhanced.

Were the monopoly abolished, it would be impossible for the Government efficiently to check the contraband importation of so easily smuggled an article as prepared opium, or *chandu*, and by lowering the price the consumption would be increased.

The use of the drug is almost entirely confined to the Chinese portion of the population. A poll-tax, customs and excise duties, mining royalties and fines and fees make up the rest of the revenue, which in 1884 amounted to $237,752 and in 1885 to $315,264. The expenditure for the same years is given by Vice-Consul CADELL as $234,161 and $321,264, respectively. In the early days of Sarawak, it was a very serious problem to find the money to pay the expenses of a most economical Government. Sir JAMES BROOKE sunk all his own fortune—£30,000—in the country, and took so gloomy a view of the financial prospects of his kingdom that, on the refusal of England to annex it, he offered it first to France and then to Holland. Fortunately these offers were never carried into effect, and, with the assistance of the Borneo Company (not to be confused with the British North Borneo Company), who acquired the concession of the right to work the minerals in Sarawak, bad times were tided over, and, by patient perseverance, the finances of the State have been brought to their present satisfactory condition. What the amount of the national public debt is, I am not in a position to say, but, like all other countries aspiring to be civilized, it possesses a small one. The improvement in the financial position was undoubtedly chiefly due to the influx of Chinese, especially of gambier and pepper planters, who were attracted by liberal concessions of land and monetary assistance in the first instance from the Government. The present Raja has himself said that "without the Chinese we can do nothing," and we have only to turn to the British possession in the far East—the Straits Settlements, the Malay Peninsula, and Hongkong—to see that this is the case. For instance, the revenue of the Straits Settlements in 1887 was $3,847,475, of which the opium farm alone—that is a tax practically speaking borne by the Chinese population—contributed $1,779,600, or not very short of one half of the whole, and they of course contribute in many other ways as well. The frugal, patient, industrious, go-ahead, money-making Chinaman is undoubtedly the colonist for the sparsely inhabited islands of the Malay archipelago. Where, as in Java, there is a large native population and the struggle for existence has compelled the natives to adopt habits of industry, the presence of the Chinaman is not a necessity, but in a country like Borneo, where the inhabitants, from time immemorial, except during unusual periods of drought or epidemic sickness, have never found the problem of existence bear hard upon them, it is impossible to impress upon the natives that they ought to have "wants," whether they feel them or not, and that the pursuit of the dollar for the sake of mere possession is an ennobling object, differentiating the simple savage from the complicated product of the higher civilization. The Malay, in his ignorance, thinks that if he can obtain clothing suitable to the climate, a hut which adequately protects him from sun and rain, and a wife to be the mother of his children and the cooker of his meals, he should therewith rest content; but, then, no country made up of units possessed of this simple faith can ever come to anything—can ever be civilized, and hence the necessity for the Chinese immigrant in Eastern Colonies that want to shew an annual revenue advancing by leaps and bounds. The Chinaman, too, in addition to his valuable properties as a keen trader and a man of business, collecting from the natives the products of the country, which he passes on to the European merchant, from whom he obtains the European fabrics and American "notions" to barter with the natives, is also a good agriculturist, whether on a large or small scale; he is muscular and can endure both heat and cold, and so is, at any rate in the tropics, far and away a superior animal to the white labourer, whether for agricultural or mining work, as an artizan, or as a hewer of wood and drawer of water, as a cook, a housemaid or a washerwoman. He can learn any trade that a white man can teach him, from ship-building to watchmaking, and he does not drink and requires scarcely any holidays or Sundays, occasionally only a day to worship his ancestors.

It will be said that if he does not drink he smokes opium. Yes! he does, and this, as we have seen, is what makes him so beloved of the Colonial Chancellors of the Exchequer. At the same time he is, if strict justice and firmness are shewn him, wonderfully law-abiding and orderly. Faction fights, and serious ones no doubt, do occur between rival classes and rival secret societies, but to nothing like the extent that would be the case were they white men. It is not, I think, sufficiently borne in mind, that a very large proportion of the Chinese there are of the lower, I may say of the lowest, orders, many of them of the criminal class and the scourings of some of the large cities of China, who arrive at their destination in possession of nothing but a pair of trowsers and a jacket and,

may be, an opium pipe ; in addition to this they come from
different provinces, between the inhabitants of which there
has always been rivalry, and the languages of which are so
entirely different that it is a usual thing to find Chinese of
different provinces compelled to carry on their conversation
in Malay or "pidgeon" English, and finally, as though the
elements of danger were not already sufficient, they are
pressed on their arrival to join rival secret societies, between
which the utmost enmity and hatred exists. Taking all these
things into consideration, I maintain that the Chinaman is a
good and orderly citizen and that his good qualities, especially
as a revenue-payer in the Far East, much more than counter-
balance his bad ones. The secret societies, whose organiza-
tion permeates Chinese society from the top to the bottom,
are the worst feature in the social condition of the Chinese
colonists, and in Sarawak a summary method of suppressing
them has been adopted. The penalty for belonging to one of
these societies is death. When Sir JAMES BROOKE took over
Sarawak, there was a considerable Chinese population, settled
for generations in the country and recruited from Dutch territory, where they had been subject to no supervision by the
Government, whose hold over the country was merely nominal. They were principally gold diggers, and being accustomed
to manage their own affairs and settle their disputes amongst
themselves, they resented any interference from the new
rulers, and, in 1857, a misunderstanding concerning the opium
revenue having occurred, they suddenly rose in arms and
seized the capital. It was some time before the Raja's
forces could be collected and let loose upon them, when large
numbers were killed and the majority of the survivors took
refuge in Dutch territory.

The scheme for introducing Chinese pepper and gambier
planters into Sarawak was set on foot in 1878 or 1879, and
has proved a decided success, though, as Vice-Consul CADELL
remarked in 1886, it is difficult to understand why even
larger numbers have not availed themselves of the terms
offered "since coolies have the protection of the Sarawak
Government, which further grants them free passages from
Singapore, whilst the climate is a healthy one, and there are

no dangers to be feared from wild animals, tigers being unknown in Sarawak." The fact remains that, though there is plenty of available land, there is an insufficiency of Chinese labour still. The quantity of pepper exported in 1885 was 392 tons, valued at £19,067, and of gambier 1,370 tons, valued at £23,772.

Sarawak is said to supply more than half of the sago produce of the world. The value of the sago it exported in 1885 is returned at £35,953. Of the purely uncultivated jungle products that figure in the exports the principal are guttapercha, India rubber, and rattans.

Both antimony ores and cinnabar (an ore of quicksilver) are worked by the Borneo Company, but the exports of the former ore and of quicksilver are steadily decreasing, and fresh deposits are being sought for. Only one deposit of cinnabar has so far been discovered, that was in 1867. Antimony was first discovered in Sarawak in 1824, and for a long time it was from this source that the principal supplies for Europe and America were obtained. The ores are found "generally as boulders deep in clayey soil, or perched on tower-like summits and craggy pinnacles and, sometimes, in dykes *in situ*." The ores, too poor for shipment, are reduced locally, and the *regulus* exported to London. Coal is abundant, but is not yet worked on any considerable scale.* The Borneo Company excepted, all the trade of the country is in the hands of Chinese and Natives, nor has the Government hitherto taken steps to attract European capital for planting, but expirements are being made with the public funds under European supervision in the planting of cinchona, coffee, and tobacco. The capital of Sarawak is *Kuching*, which in Malay signifies a "cat." It is situated about fifteen miles up the Sarawak river and, when Sir JAMES first arrived, was a wretched native town, with palm leaf huts and a population, including a few Chinese and Klings (natives of India), of some two thousand. Kuching now possesses a well built "Istana," or Palace of the Raja, a Fort, impregnable to natives, a substan-

---

* Since this was written, Raja Sir CHARLES BROOKE has acquired valuable coal concessions at Muara, at the mouth of the Brunai river, and the development of the coal resources of the State is being energetically pushed forward.

tial Gaol, Court House, Government Offices, Public Market and Church, and is the headquarters of the Bishop of Singapore and Sarawak, who is the head of the Protestant Mission in the country. There is a well built brick Chinese trading quarter, or "bazaar," the Europeans have comfortable bungalows, and the present population is said to number twelve thousand.

In the early days of his reign, Sir JAMES BROOKE was energetically assisted in his great work of suppressing piracy and rendering the seas and rivers safe for the passage of the peaceful trader, by the British men-of-war on the China Station, and was singularly fortunate in having an energetic co-adjutor in Captain (now Admiral) Sir HENRY KEPPEL, K.C.B.

It will give some idea of the extent to which piracy, then almost the sole occupation of the Illanun, Balinini, and Sea Dyak tribes, was indulged in that the "Headmoney," then paid by the British Government for pirates destroyed, amounted in these expeditions to the large total of £20,000, the awarding of which sum occasioned a great stir at the time and led to the abolition of this system of "payment by results." Mr. HUME took exception altogether to the action of Sir JAMES BROOKE, and, in 1851, charges were brought against him, and a Royal Commission appointed to take evidence on the spot, or rather at Singapore.

A man like BROOKE, of an enthusiastic, impulsive, unselfish and almost Quixotic disposition, who wore his heart on his sleeve and let his opinions of men and their actions be freely known, could not but have incurred the enmity of many meaner, self-seeking minds. The Commission, after hearing all that could be brought against him, found that there was nothing proved, but it was not deemed advisable that Sir JAMES should continue to act as the British representative in Borneo and as Governor of the Colony of Labuan, positions which were indeed incompatible with that of the independent ruler of Sarawak. Sarawak independence was first recognised by the Americans, and the British followed suit in 1863, when a Vice-Consulate was established there. The question of formally proclaiming a British Protectorate over Sarawak is now being

considered, and it is to be hoped, will be carried into effect.*
The *personel* of the Government is purely British, most of
the merchants and traders are of British nationality, and the
whole trade of the country finds its way to the British Colony
of the Straits Settlements.

We can scarely let a country such as this, with its local and
other resources, so close to Singapore and on the route to
China, fall into the hands of any other European Power, and
the only means of preventing such a catastrophe is by the proclamation of a Protectorate over it—a Protectorate which, so
long as the successors of Raja BROOKE prove their compe-
tence to govern, should be worked so as to interfere as little
as possible in the internal affairs of the State. The virulently
hostile and ignorant criticisms to which Sir JAMES BROOKE was
subjected in England, and the financial difficulties of this little
kingdom, coupled with a serious dispute with a nephew whom
he had appointed his successor, but whom he was compelled
to depose, embittered the last years of his life. To the end
he fought his foes in his old, plucky, honest, vigorous and
straightforward style. He died in June, 1868, from a paraly-
tic stroke, and was succeeded by his nephew, the present
Raja. What Sir JAMES BROOKE might have accomplished
had he not been hampered by an opposition based on ignorance and imperfect knowledge at home, we cannot say; what
he did achieve, I have endeavoured briefly to sketch, and unprejudiced minds cannot but deem the founding of a prosperous State and the total extirpation of piracy, slavery and
head-hunting, a monument worthy of a high, noble and unselfish nature.

In addition to that of the Church of England, there has,
within the last few years, been established a Roman Catholic
Mission, under the auspices of the St. Joseph's College, Mill Hill.

The Muhammadans, including all the true Malay inhabitants,
do not make any concerted effort to disseminate the doctrines
of their faith.

The following information relative to the Church of England Mission has been kindly furnished me by the Right

---

* This has since been formally proclaimed.

Reverend Dr. HOSE, the present Bishop of "Singapore, Labuan and Sarawak," which is the official title of his extensive See which includes the Colony of the Straits Settlements—Penang, Province Wellesley, Malacca and Singapore—and its Dependencies, the Protected States of the Malay Peninsula, the State of Sarawak, the Crown Colony of Labuan, the Territories of the British North Borneo Company and the Congregation of English people scattered over Malaya.

The Mission was, in the first instance, set on foot by the efforts of Lady BURDETT-COUTTS and others in 1847, when Sir JAMES BROOKE was in England and his doings in the Far East had excited much interest and enthusiasm, and was specially organized under the name of the "Borneo Church Mission." The late Reverend T. MCDOUGALL, was the first Missionary, and subsequently became the first Bishop. His name was once well known, owing to a wrong construction put upon his action, on one occasion, in making use of fire arms when a vessel, on which he was aboard, came across a fleet of pirates. He was a gifted, practical and energetic man and had the interest of his Mission at heart, and, in addition to other qualifications, added the very useful one, in his position, of being a qualified medical man. Bishop MCDOUGALL was succeeded on his retirement by Bishop CHAMBERS, who had experience gained while a Missionary in the country. The present Bishop was appointed in 1881. The Mission was eventually taken over by the Society for the Propagation of the Gospel, and this Society defrays, with unimportant exceptions, the whole cost of the See.

Dr. HOSE has under him in Sarawak eight men in holy orders, of whom six are Europeans, one Chinese and one Eurasian. The influence of the Missionaries has spread over the Skerang, Balau and Sibuyan tribes of *Sea*-Dyaks, and also among the *Land*-Dyaks near Kuching, the Capital, and among the Chinese of that town and the neighbouring pepper plantations.

There are now seven churches and twenty-five Mission chaples in Sarawak, and about 4,000 baptized Christians of the Church of England. The Mission also provides means of education and, through its press, publishes translations of the Bible, the Prayer Book and other religious and educational works, in Malay and in two Dyak dialects, which latter have only become written languages since the establishment of the Mission. In their Boys' School, at Kuching, over a hundred boys are under instruction by an English Master, assisted by a staff of Native Assistants; there is also a Girls' School, under a European Mistress, and schools at all the Mission Stations. The Government of Sarawak allows a small grant-in-aid to the schools and a salary of £200 a year to one of the Missionaries, who acts as Government Chaplain.

The Roman Catholic Mission commenced its works in Sarawak in 1881, and is under the direction of the Reverend Father JACKSON, Prefect Apostolic, who has also two or three Missionaries employed in British North Borneo. In Sarawak there are six or eight European priests and schoolmasters and a sisterhood of four or five nuns. In Kuching they have a Chapel and School and a station among the Land-Dyaks in the vicinity. They have recently established a station and erected a Chapel on the Kanowit River, an affluent of the Rejang. The Missionaries are mostly foreigners and, I believe, are under a vow to spend the remainder of their days in the East, without returning to Europe.

Their only reward is their consciousness of doing, or trying to do good, and any surplus of their meagre stipends which remains, after providing the barest necessaries of life, is refunded to the Society. I do not know what success is attending them in Sarawak, but in British North Borneo and Labuan, where they found that Father QUARTERON'S labours had left scarcely any impression, their efforts up to present have met with little success, and experiments in several rivers have had to be abandoned, owing to the utter carelessness of the Pagan natives as to matters relating to religion. When I left North Borneo in 1887, their only station which appeared to show a prospect of success was one under Father PUNDLEIDER, amongst the semi-Chinese of Bundu, to whom reference has been made on a previous page. But these people, while permitting their children to be educated and baptized by the

Father, did not think it worth their while to join the Church themselves.

Neither Mission has attempted to convert the Muhammadan tribes, and indeed it would, at present, be perfectly useless to do so and, from the Government point of view, impolitic and inadvisable as well.

CHAPTER V.

I will now take a glance at the incident of the rebellion of the inhabitants of the Limbang, the important river near Brunai to which allusion has already been made, as from this one sample he will be able to judge of the ordinary state of affairs in districts near the Capital, since the establishment of Labuan as a Crown Colony and the conclusion of the treaty and the appointment of a British Consul-General in Brunai, and will also be able to attempt to imagine the oppression prevalent before those events took place. The river, being a fertile and well populated one and near Brunai, had been from old times the common purse of the numerous nobles who, either by inheritance, or in virtue of their official positions, as I have explained, owned as their followers the inhabitants of the various villages situated on its banks, and many were the devices employed to extort the uttermost farthing from the unfortunate people, who were quite incapable of offering any resistance because the warlike Kyan tribe was ever ready at hand to sweep down upon them at the behest of their Brunai oppressors. The system of *dagang sera* (forced trade) I have already explained. Some of the other devices I will now enumerate. *Chukei basoh batis*, or the tax of washing feet, a contribution, varying in amount at the sweet will of the imposer, levied when the lord of the village, or his chief agent, did it the honour of a visit. *Chukei bongkar-sauh*, or tax on weighing anchor, similarly levied when the lord took his departure and perhaps therefore, paid with more willingness. *Chukei tolongan*, or tax of assistance, levied when the lord had need of funds for some special purpose or on a special occasion such as a wedding—and these are numerous amongst polygamists—a birth, the building of a house or of a vessel. *Chop bibas*, literally a free seal; this was a permission granted by the Sultan to some noble and needy favourite to levy a contribution for his own use anywhere he thought he could most easily enforce it. The method of inventing imaginary crimes and delinquencies and punishing them with heavy fines has been already mentioned. Then there are import and export duties as to which no reasonable complaint can be made, but a real grievance and hindrance to legitimate trade was the effort which the Malays, supported by their rulers, made to prevent the interior tribes trading direct with the Chinese and other foreign traders—acting themselves as middlemen, so that but a very small share of profit fell to the aborigines. The lords, too, had the right of appointing as many *orang kayas*, or headmen, from among the natives as they chose, a present being expected on their elevation to that position and another on their death. In many rivers there was also an annual poll-tax, but this does not appear to have been collected in the Limbang. Sir SPENCER ST.JOHN, writing in 1856, gives, in his "Life in the Forests of the Far East," several instances of the grievous oppression practiced on the Limbang people. Amongst others he mentions how a native, in a fit of desperation, had killed an extortionate tax-gatherer. Instead of having the offender arrested and punished, the Sultan ordered his village to be attacked, when fifty persons were killed and an equal number of women and children were made prisoners and kept as slaves by His Highness. The immediate cause of the rebellion to which I am now referring was the extraordinary extortion practised by one of the principal Ministers of State. The revenues of his office were principally derived from the Limbang River and, as the Sultan was very old, he determined to make the best possible use of the short time remaining to him to extract all he could from his wretched feudatories. To aid him in his design, he obtained, with the assistance of the British North Borneo Company, a steam launch, and the Limbang people subsequently pointed out to me this launch and complained bitterly that it was with the money forced out of them that this means of oppressing them had been purchased. He then employed the most uncrupulous agents he could discover, imposed outrageous fines for trifling offences, and would even interfere if he heard of any private disputes among the villagers, adjudicate unasked in their cases, taking care always to inflict a heavy fine which went, not to the party aggrieved, but into his own pocket. If the fines could not be paid, and this was often the case, owing to their being purposely fixed at such a high rate, the delinquent's sago plantations—the principal wealth of the people in the Limbang River—would be confiscated and became the private property of the Minister, or of some of the members of his household. The patience of the people was at length exhausted, and they remembered that the Brunai nobles could no longer call in the Kayans to enforce their exactions, that tribe having become subjects to Raja BROOKE. About the month of August, 1884, two of the Minister's messengers, or tax collectors, who were engaged in the usual process of squeezing the people, were fired on and killed by the Bisayas, the principal pagan tribe in the river. The Tumonggong determined to punish this outrage in person and probably thought his august presence on the spot in a steam-launch, would quickly bring the natives to their knees and afford him a grand opportunity of replenishing his treasury.

He accordingly ascended the river with a considerable force in September, and great must have been his surprise when he found that his messenger, sent in advance to call the people to meet him, was fired on and killed. He could scarcely have believed the evidence of his own ears, however, when shortly afterwards his royal launch and little fleet were fired on from the river banks. For two days was this firing kept up, the Brunais having great difficulty in returning it, owing to the river being low and the banks steep and lined with large trees, behind which the natives took shelter, and, a few casualties having occurred on board and one of the Royal guns having burst, which was known as the *Amiral Muminin*, the Tumonggong deemed it expedient to retire and returned ignominiously to Brunai. The rebels, emboldened by the impunity they had so far enjoyed, were soon found to be hovering round the outskirts of the capital, and every now and then an outlying house would be attacked during the night and the headless corpses of its occupants be found on the morrow. There being no forts and no organized force to resist attack, the houses, moreover, being nearly all constructed of highly inflammable palm leaf thatch and matting, a universal panic prevailed amongst all classes, when the Limbang people announced their intention of firing the town. Considerable distress too prevailed, as the spirit of rebellion had spread to all the districts near the capital, and the Brunai people who had settled in them were compelled to flee for their lives, leaving their property in the hands of the insurgents, while the people of the city were unable to follow their usual avocations—trading, planting, sago washing and so forth, the Brunai River, as has been pointed out, producing nothing itself. British trade being thus affected by the continuance of such a state of affairs, and the British subjects in the city being in daily fear from the apprehended attack by the rebels, the English Consul-General did what he could to try and arrange matters. A certain Datu KLASSIE, one of the most influential of the Bisaya Chiefs, came into Brunai without any followers, but bringing with him, as a proof of the friendliness of his mission, his wife. Instead of utilizing the services of this Chief in opening communication with the natives, the Tumonggong, maddened by his ignominious defeat, seized both Datu KLASSIE and his wife and placed them in the public stocks, heavily ironed.

I was Acting Consul-General at the time, and my assistance in arranging matters had been requested by the Brunai Government, while the Bisayas also had expressed their warm desire to meet and consult with me if I would trust myself amongst them, and I at once arranged so to do; but, being well aware that my mission would be perfectly futile unless I was the bearer of terms from the Sultan and unless Datu KLASSIE and his wife were released, I refused to take any steps until these two points were conceded..

This was a bitter pill for the Brunai Rajas and especially for the Tumonggong, who, though perfectly aware that he was quite unable, not only to punish the rebels, but even to defend the city against their attacks, yet clung to the vain hope that the British Government might be induced to regard them as pirates and so interfere in accordance with the terms of the treaty, or that the Raja of Sarawak would construe some old agreement made with Sir JAMES BROOKE as necessitating his rendering armed assistance.

However, owing to the experience, tact, perseverance and intelligence of Inche MAHOMET, the Consular Agent, we gained our point after protracted negotiations, and obtained the seals of the Sultan, the Bandahara, the Di Gadong and the Tumonggong himself to a document, by which it was provided that, on condition of the Limbang people laying down their arms and allowing free intercourse with Brunai, all arbitrary taxation such as that which has been described should be for ever abolished, but that, in lieu therefor, a fixed poll-tax should be paid by all adult males, at the rate of $3 per annum by married men and $2 by bachelors; that on the death of an *orang kaya* the contribution to be paid to the feudal lord should be fixed at one pikul of brass gun, equal to about $21; that the possession of their sago plantations should be peaceably enjoyed by their owners; that jungle products should be collected without tax, except in the case of gutta percha, on which a royalty of 5% *ad valorem* should be paid, instead of the 20% then exacted; that the taxes should be collected by the headmen punctually and transmitted to Brunai, and that four Brunai tax-gatherers, who were mentioned by name and whose rapacious and criminal action had been instrumental in provoking the rebellion, should be forbidden ever again to enter the Limbang River; that a free pardon should be granted to the rebels.

Accompanied by Inche MAHOMET and with some Bisaya interpreters, I proceeded up the Limbang River, on the 21st October, in a steam-launch, towing the boats of Pangeran ISTRI NAGARA and of the Datu AHAMAT, who were deputed to accompany us and represent the Brunai Government.

Several hundred of the natives assembled to meet us, and the Government conditions were read out and explained. It was evident that the people found it difficult to place much reliance in the promises of the Rajas, although the document was formally attested by the seals of the Sultan and of his three Ministers, and a duplicate had been prepared for them to keep in their custody for future reference. It was seen, too, that there were a number of Muhammadans in the crowd who appeared adverse to the acceptance of the terms offered, and, doubtless, many of them were acting at the instigation of the Tumonggong's party, who by no means relished so peaceful a solution of the difficulties their chief's action had brought about.

Whilst the conference was still going on and the various clauses of the *firman* were being debated, news arrived that the Rajas had, in the basest manner, let loose the Trusan Muruts on the district the day we had sailed for the Limbang, and that these wretches had murdered and carried off the heads of four women, two of whom were pregnant, and two young unmarried girls and of two men who were at work in their gardens.

This treacherous action was successful in breaking up the meeting, and was not far from causing the massacre of at any rate the Brunai portion of our party, and the Pangeran and the Datu quickly betook themselves to their boats and scuttled off to Brunai not waiting for the steam-launch.

But we determined not to be beaten by the Rajas' manœuvres, and so, though a letter reached me from the Sultan warning me of what had occurred and urging me to return to Brunai, we stuck to our posts, and ultimately were rewarded by the Bisayas returning and the majority of their principal chiefs signing, or rather marking the document embodying their new constitution, as it might be termed, in token of their acquiescence—a result which should be placed to the credit of the indefatigable Inche MAHOMET, whose services I am happy to say were specially recognised in a despatch from the Foreign Office. Returning to Brunai, I demanded the release of Datu KLASSIE, as had been agreed upon, but it was only after I had made use of very plain language to his messengers that the Tumonggong gave orders for his release and that of his wife, whom I had the pleasure of taking up the river and restoring to their friends.

H. M. S. *Pegasus* calling at Labuan soon afterwards, I seized the opportunity to request Captain BICKFORD to make a little demonstration in Brunai, which was not often visited by a man-of-war, with the double object of restoring confidence to the British subjects there and the traders generally and of exacting a public apology for the disgraceful conduct of the Government in allowing the Muruts to attack the Limbang people while we were up that river. Captain BICKFORD at once complied with my request, and, as the *Pegasus* drew too much water to cross the bar, the boats were manned and armed and towed up to the city by a steam-launch. It was rather a joke against me that the launch which towed up the little flotilla designed to overawe Brunai was sent for the occasion by one of the principal Ministers of the Sultan. It was placed at my disposal by the Pangeran Di Gadong, who was then a bitter enemy of the Tumonggong, and glad to witness his discomfiture. This was on the 3rd November, 1884.

With reference to the heads taken on the occasion mentioned above, I may add that the Muruts were allowed to retain them, and the disgusting sight was to be seen, at one of the watering places in the town, of these savages "cooking" and preparing the heads for keeping in their houses.

As the Brunai Government was weak and powerless, I am of opinion that the agreement with the Limbang people might have been easily worked had the British Government thought it worth while to insist upon its observance. As it was, hostilities did cease, the headmen came down and visited the old Sultan, and trade recommenced. In June, 1885, Sultan MUMIM died, at the age, according to Native statements, which are very unreliable on such points, of 114 years, and was succeeded by the Tumonggong, who was proclaimed Sultan on the 5th June of the same year, when I had the honour of being present at the ceremony, which was not of an imposing character. The new Sultan did not forget the mortifying treatment he had received at the hands of the Limbang people, and refused to receive their Chiefs. He retained, too, in his own hands the appointment of Tumonggong, and with it the rights of that office over the Limbang River, and it became the interest of many different parties to prevent the completion of the pacification of that district. The gentleman for whom I had been acting as Consul-General soon afterwards returned to his post. In May, 1887, Sir FREDERICK WELD, Governor of the Straits Settlements, was despatched to Brunai by Her Majesty's Government, on a special mission, to report on the affairs of the Brunai Sultanate and as to recent cessions of territory made, or in course of negotiation, to the British North Borneo Company and to Sarawak. His report has not been yet made public. There were at one time grave objections to allowing Raja BROOKE to extend his territory, as there was no guarantee that some one of his successors might not prefer a life of inglorious ease in England to the task of governing natives in the tropics, and sell his kingdom to the highest bidder—say France or Germany; but if the British Protectorate over Sarawak is formally proclaimed, there would appear to be no reasonable objection to the BROOKES establishing their Government in such other districts as the Sultan may see good of his own free will to cede, but it should be the duty of the British Government to see that their ally is fairly treated and that any cessions he may make are entirely voluntary and not brought about by coercion in any form—direct or indirect.

CHAPTER VI.

The British Colony of Labuan was obtained by cession from the Sultan of Brunai and was in the shape of a *quid pro quo* for assistance in suppressing piracy in the neighbouring seas, which the Brunai Government was supposed to have at heart, but in all probability, the real reason of the willingness on the Sultan's part to cede it was his desire to obtain a powerful ally to assist him in reasserting his authority in many parts of the North and West portions of his dominions, where the allegiance of the people had been transferred to the Sultan of Sulu and to Illanun and Balinini piratical leaders. It was a similar reason which, in 1774, induced the Brunai Government to grant to the East India Company the monopoly of the trade in pepper, and is explained in Mr. JESSE'S letter to the Court of Directors as follows. He says that he found the reason of their unanimous inclination to cultivate the friendship and alliance of the Company was their desire for

" protection from their piratical neighbours, the Sulus and Mindanaos, and others, who make continual depredations on their coast, by taking advantage of their natural timidity."

The first connection of the British with Labuan was on the occasion of their being expelled by the Sulus from Balambangan, in 1775, when they took temporary refuge on the island.

In 1844, Captain Sir EDWARD BELCHER visited Brunai to enquire into rumours of the detention of a European female in the country—rumours which proved to be unfounded. Sir JAMES BROOKE accompanied him, and on this occasion the Sultan, who had been terrified by a report that his capital was to be attacked by a British squadron of sixteen or seventeen vessels, addressed a document, in conjunction with Raja Muda HASSIM, to the Queen of England, requesting her aid "for the suppression of piracy and the encouragement and extension of trade; and to assist in forwarding these objects they are willing to cede, to the Queen of England, the Island of Labuan, and its islets on such terms as may hereafter be arranged by any person appointed by Her Majesty. The Sultan and the Raja Muda HASSIM consider that an English Settlement on Labuan will be of great service to the natives of the coast, and will draw a considerable trade from the northward, and from China; and should Her Majesty the Queen of England decide upon the measure, the Sultan and the Raja Muda HASSIM promise to afford every assistance to the English authorities." In February of the following year, the Sultan and Raja Muda HASSIM, in a letter accepting Sir JAMES BROOKE as Her Majesty's Agent in Borneo, without specially mentioning Labuan, expressed their adherence to their former declarations, conveyed through Sir EDWARD BELCHER, and asked for immediate assistance "to protect Borneo from the pirates of Marudu," a Bay situated at the northern extremity of Borneo—assistance which was rendered in the following August, when the village of Marudu was attacked and destroyed, though it is perhaps open to doubt whether the chief, OSMAN, quite deserved the punishment he received. On the 1st March of the same year (1845) the Sultan verbally asked Sir JAMES BROOKE whether and at what time the English proposed to take possession of Labuan. Then followed the episode already narrated of the murder by the Sultan of Raja Muda HASSIM and his family and the taking of Brunai by Admiral COCHRANE'S Squadron. In November, 1846, instructions were received in Singapore, from Lord PALMERSTON, to take possession of Labuan, and Captain RODNEY MUNDY was selected for this service. He arrived in Brunai in December, and gives an amusing account of how he proceeded to carry out his orders and obtain the *voluntary* cession of the island. As a preliminary, he sent "Lieutenant " LITTLE in charge of the boats of the *Iris* and *Wolf*, armed " with twenty marines, to the capital, with orders to moor " them in line of battle opposite the Sultan's palace, and to " await my arrival." On reaching the palace, Captain MUNDY produced a brief document, to which he requested the Sultan to affix his seal, and which provided for eternal friendship between the two countries, and for the cession of Labuan, in consideration of which the Queen engaged to use her best endeavours to suppress piracy and protect lawful commerce. The document of 1844 had stated that Labuan would be ceded "on such terms as may hereafter be arranged," and a promise to suppress piracy, the profits in which were shared by the Sultan and his nobles, was by no means regarded by them as a fair set off; it was a condition with which they would have readily dispensed. The Sultan ventured to remark that the present treaty was different to the previous one, and that a money payment was required in exchange for the cession of territory. Captain MUNDY replied that the former treaty had been broken when Her Majesty's Ships were fired on by the Brunai forts, and "at last I turned to the Sultan, and exclaimed firmly, 'Bobo chop bobo chop!' followed up by a few other Malay words, the tenor of which was, that I recommended His Majesty to put his seal forthwith." And he did so. Captain MUNDY hoisted the British Flag at Labuan on the 24th December, 1846, and there still exists at Labuan in the place where it was erected by the gallant Captain, a granite slab, with an inscription recording the fact of the formal taking possession of the island in Her Majesty's name.

In the following year, Sir JAMES BROOKE was appointed the first Governor of the new Colony, retaining his position as the British representative in Brunai, and being also the ruler of Sarawak, the independence of which was not formally recognised by the English Government until the year 1863. Sir JAMES was assisted at Labuan by a Lieutenant-Governor and staff of European Officers, who on their way through Singapore are said to have somewhat offended the susceptibilities of the Officials of that Settlement by pointing to the fact that they were Queen's Officers, whereas the Straits Settlements were at that time still under the Government of the East India Company. Sir JAMES BROOKE held the position of Governor until 1851, and the post has since been filled by such well-known administrators as Sir HUGH LOW, Sir JOHN POPE HENNESSY, Sir HENRY E. BULWER and Sir CHARLES LEES, but the expectations formed at its foundation have never been realized and the little Colony appears to be in a moribund condition, the Governorship having been left unfilled since 1881. On the 27th May, 1847, Sir JAMES BROOKE concluded the Treaty with the Sultan of Brunai which is still in force. Labuan is situated off the mouth of the Brunai River and has an area of thirty square miles. It was uninhabited when we took it, being only occasionally visited by fishermen. It was then covered, like all tropical countries, whether the soil is rich or poor, with dense forest, some of the trees being valuable as timber, but most of this has since been destroyed, partly by the successive coal companies, who required large quantities of timber for their mines, but chiefly by the destructive mode of cultivation practised by the Kadyans and other squatters from Borneo, who were allowed to destroy the forest for a crop or two of rice, the soil, except in the flooded plains, being not rich enough to carry more than one or two such harvests under such primitive methods of agriculture as only are known to the natives. The lands so cleared were deserted and were soon covered with a strong growth of fern and coarse useless *lalang* grass, difficult to eradicate, and it is well known that, when a tropical forest is once destroyed and the land left to itself, the new jungle which may in time spring up rarely contains any of the valuable timber trees which composed the original forest.

A few cargoes of timber were also exported by Chinese to Hongkong. Great hopes were entertained that the establishment of a European Government and a free port on an island lying alongside so rich a country as Borneo would result in its becoming an emporium and collecting station for the various products of, at any rate, the northern and western portions of this country and perhaps, too, of the Sulu Archipelago. Many causes prevented the realization of these hopes. In the first place, no successful efforts were made to restore good government on the mainland, and without a fairly good government and safety to life and property, trade could not be developed. Then again Labuan was overshaded by the prosperous Colony of Singapore, which is the universal emporium for all these islands, and, with the introduction of steamers, it was soon found that only the trade of the coast immediately opposite to Labuan could be depended upon, that of the rest' including Sarawak and the City of Brunai, going direct to Singapore, for which port Labuan became a subsidiary and unimportant collecting station. The Spanish authorities did what they could to prevent trade with the Sulu Islands, and, on the signing of the Protocol between that country and Great Britain and Germany freeing the trade from restrictions, Sulu produce has been carried by steamers direct to Singapore. Since 1881, the British North Borneo Company having opened ports to the North, the greater portion of the trade of their possessions likewise finds its way direct by steamers to the same port.

Labuan has never shipped cargoes direct to England, and its importance as a collecting station for Singapore is now diminishing, for the reasons above-mentioned.

Most or a large portion of the trade that now falls to its share comes from the southern portion of the British North Borneo Company's territories, from which it is distant, at the nearest point, only about six miles, and the most reasonable solution of the Labuan question would certainly appear to be the proclamation of a British Protectorate over North Borneo, to which, under proper guarantees, might be assigned the task of carrying on the government of Labuan, a task which it could easily and economically undertake, having a sufficiently well organised staff ready to hand.* By the Royal Charter it is already provided that the appointment of the Company's Governor in Borneo is subject to the sanction of Her Majesty's Secretary of State, and the two Officers hitherto selected have been Colonial servants, whose service have been *lent* by the Colonial Office to the Company.

The Census taken in 1881 gives the total population of Labuan as 5,995, but it has probably decreased considerably since that time. The number of Chinese supposed to be settled there is about 300 or 400—traders, shopkeepers, coolies and sago-washers; the preparation of sago flour from the raw sago, or *lamuntah*, brought in from the mainland by the natives, being the principal industry of the island and employing three or four factories, in which no machinery is used. All the traders are only agents of Singapore firms and are in a small way of business. There is no European firm, or shop, in the island. Coal of good quality for raising steam is plentiful, especially at the North end of the island, and very sanguine expectations of the successful working of these coal measures were for a long time entertained, but have hitherto not been realised. The Eastern Archipelago Company, with an ambitious title but too modest an exchequer, first attempted to open the mines soon after the British occupation, but failed, and has been succeeded by three others, all I believe Scotch, the last one stopping operations in 1878. The cause of failure seems to have been the same in each case—insufficient capital, local mismanagement, difficulty in obtaining labour. In a country with a rainfall of perhaps over 120 inches a year, water was naturally another difficulty in the deep workings. but this might have been very easily overcome had the Companies been in a position to purchase sufficiently powerful pumping engines.

There were three workable seams of coal, one of them, I think, twelve feet in thickness; the quality of the coal, though

---

* My suggestion has taken shape more quickly than I expected. In 1889 Labuan was put under the administration of the Company.

inferior to Welsh, was superior to Australian, and well reported on by the engineers of many steamers which had tried it; the vessels of the China squadron and the numerous steamers engaged in the Far East offered a ready market for the coal.

In their effort to make a "show," successive managers have pretty nearly exhausted the surface workings and so honeycombed the seams with their different systems of developing their resources, that it would be, perhaps, a difficult and expensive undertaking for even a substantial company to make much of them now.*

It is needless to add that the failure to develop this one internal resource of Labuan was a great blow to the Colony, and on the cessation of the last company's operations the revenue immediately declined, a large number of workmen—European, Chinese and Natives—being thrown out of employment, necessitating the closing of the shops in which they spent their wages. It was found that both Chinese and the Natives of Borneo proved capital miners under European supervision.

Notwithstanding the ill-luck that has attended it, the little Colony has not been a burden on the British tax-payer since the year 1860, but has managed to collect a revenue—chiefly from opium, tobacco, spirits, pawnbroking and fish "farms" and from land rents and land sales—sufficient to meet its small expenditure, at present about £4,000 a year. There have been no British troops quartered in this island since 1871, and the only armed force is the Native Constabulary, numbering, I think, a dozen rank and file. Very seldom are the inhabitants cheered by the welcome visit of a British gunboat. Still, all the formality of a British Crown Colony is kept up. The administrator is by his subjects styled "His Excellency" and the Members of the Legislative Council, Native and Europeans, are addressed as the "Honourable so and so." An Officer, as may be supposed, has to play many parts. The present Treasurer, for instance, is an ex-Lieutenant of

---

* Since the above was written, a fifth company—the Central Borneo Company, Limited, of London—has taken in hand the Labuan coal and, finding plenty of coal to work on without sinking a shaft, confidently anticipate success. Their £1 shares recently went up to £4.

Her Majesty's Navy, and is at the same time Harbour Master, Postmaster, Coroner, Police Magistrate, likewise a Judge of the Supreme Court, Superintendent of Convicts, Surveyor-General, and Clerk to the Legislative Council, and occasionally has, I believe, to write official letters of reprimand or encouragement from himself in one capacity to himself in another.

The best thing about Labuan is, perhaps, the excellence of its fruit, notably of its pumeloes, oranges and mangoes, for which the Colony is indebted to the present Sir HUGH LOW, who was one of the first officials under Sir JAMES BROOKE, and a man who left no stone unturned in his efforts to promote the prosperity of the island. His name was known far and wide in Northern Borneo and in the Sulu Archipelago. As an instance, I was once proceeding up a river in the island of Basilan, to the North of Sulu, with Captain C. E. BUCKLE, R.N., in two boats of H. M. S. *Frolic*, when the natives, whom we could not see, opened fire on us from the banks. I at once jumped up and shouted out that we were Mr. LOW's friends from Labuan, and in a very short time we were on friendly terms with the natives, who conducted us to their village. They had thought we might be Spaniards, and did not think it worth while to enquire before firing. The mention of the *Frolic* reminds me that on the termination of a somewhat lengthy cruise amongst the Sulu Islands, then nominally undergoing blockade by Spanish cruisers, we were returning to Labuan through the difficult and then only partially surveyed Malawalli Channel, and after dinner we were congratulating one another on having been so safely piloted through so many dangers, when before the words were out of our mouths, we felt a shock and found ourselves fast on an unmarked rock which has since had the honour of bearing the name of our good little vessel.

Besides Mr. LOW's fruit garden, the only other European attempt at planting was made by my Cousin, Dr. TREACHER, Colonial Surgeon, who purchased an outlying island and opened a coco-nut plantation. I regret to say that in neither case, owing to the decline of the Colony, was the enterprise of the pioneers adequately rewarded.

Labuan* at one time boasted a Colonial Chaplain and gave its name to the Bishop's See; but in 1872 or 1873, the Church was "disestablished" and the few European Officials who formed the congregation were unable to support a Clergyman. There exists a pretty little wooden Church, and the same indefatigable officer, whom I have described as filling most of the Government appointments in the Colony, now acts as unpaid Chaplain, having been licensed thereto by the Bishop of Singapore and Sarawak, and reads the service and even preaches a sermon every Sunday to a congregation which rarely numbers half a dozen.

Chapter VII.

The mode of acquisition of British North Borneo has been referred to in former pages; it was by cession for annual money payments to the Sultans of Brunai and of Sulu, who had conflicting claims to be the paramount power in the northern portion of Borneo. The actual fact was that neither of them exercised any real government or authority over by far the greater portion, the inhabitants of the coast on the various rivers following any Brunai, Illanun, Bajau, or Sulu Chief who had sufficient force of character to bring himself to the front. The pagan tribes of the interior owned allegiance to neither Sultan, and were left to govern themselves, the Muhammadan coast people considering them fair game for plunder and oppression whenever opportunity occurred, and using all their endeavours to prevent Chinese and other foreign traders from reaching them, acting themselves as middlemen, buying (bartering) at very cheap rates from the aborigines and selling for the best price they could obtain to the foreigner.

I believe I am right in saying that the idea of forming a Company, something after the manner of the East India Company, to take over and govern North Borneo, originated in the fol-

---

* The administration of this little Crown Colony has since been entrusted to the British North Borneo Company, their present Governor, Mr. C. V. CREAGH, having been gazetted Governor of Labuan.

lowing manner. In 1865 Mr. MOSES, the unpaid Consul for the United Sates in Brunai, to whom reference has been made before, acquired with his friends from the Sultan of Brunai some concessions of territory with the right to govern and collect revenues, their idea being to introduce Chinese and establish a Colony. This they attempted to carry out on a small scale in the Kimanis River, on the West Coast, but not having sufficient capital the scheme collapsed, but the concession was retained. Mr. MOSES subsequently lost his life at sea, and a Colonel TORREY became the chief representative of the American syndicate. He was engaged in business in China, where he met Baron VON OVERBECK, a merchant of Hongkong and Austrian Consul-General, and interested him in the scheme. In 1875 the Baron visited Borneo in company with the Colonel, interviewed the Sultan of Brunai, and made enquiries as to the validity of the concessions, with apparently satisfactory results. Mr. ALFRED DENT* was also a China merchant well known in Shanghai, and he in turn was interested in the idea by Baron OVERBECK. Thinking there might be something in the scheme, he provided the required capital, chartered a steamer, the *America*, and authorised Baron OVERBECK to proceed to Brunai to endeavour, with Colonel TORREY'S assistance, to induce the Sultan and his Ministers to transfer the American cessions to himself and the Baron, or rather to cancel the previous ones and make out new ones in their favour and that of their heirs, associates, successors and assigns for so long as they should choose or desire to hold them. Baron VON OVERBECK was accompanied by Colonel TORREY and a staff of three Europeans, and, on settling some arrears due by the American Company, succeeded in accomplishing the objects of his mission, after protracted and tedious negotiations, and obtained a " chop" from the Sultan nominating and appointing him supreme ruler, "with the title of Maharaja of Sabah (North Borneo) and Raja of Gaya and Sandakan, with power of life and death over the inhabitants, with all the absolute rights of

---

* Now Sir ALFRRD DENT, K.C.M.G.

property vested in the Sultan over the soil of the country, and the right to dispose of the same, as well as of the rights over the productions of the country, whether mineral, vegetable, or animal, with the rights of making laws, coining money, creating an army and navy, levying customs rates on home and foreign trade and shipping, and other dues and taxes on the inhabitants as to him might seem good or expedient, together with all other powers and rights usually exercised by and belonging to sovereign rulers, and which the Sultan thereby delegated to him of his own free will; and the Sultan called upon all foreign nations, with whom he had formed friendly treaties and alliances, to acknowledge the said Maharaja as the Sultan himself in the said territories and to respect his authority therein; and in the case of the death or retirement from the said office of the said Maharaja, then his duly appointed successor in the office of Supreme Ruler and Governor-in-Chief of the Company's territories in Borneo should likewise succeed to the office and title of Maharaja of Sabah and Raja of Gaya and Sandakan, and all the powers above enumerated be vested in him." I am quoting from the preamble to the Royal Charter. Some explanation of the term "Sabah" as applied to the territory—a term which appears in the Prayer Book version of the 72nd Psalm, verse 10, "The kings of Arabia and Sabah shall bring gifts"—seems called for, but I regret to say I have not been able to obtain a satisfactory one from the Brunai people, who use it in connection only with a small portion of the West Coast of Borneo, North of the Brunai river. Perhaps the following note, which I take from Mr. W. E. MAXWELL'S " Manual of the Malay Language," may have some slight bearing on the point :—" Sawa, Jawa, Saba, Jaba, Zaba, etc., has evidently in all times been the capital local name in Indonesia. The whole archipelago was pressed into an island of that name by the Hindus and Romans. Even in the time of MARCO POLO we have only a Java Major and a Java Minor. The Bugis apply the name of Jawa, *ja-waka* (comp. the Polynesian *Sawaiki*, Ceramese *Sawai*) to the Moluccas. One of the principal divisions of Battaland in Sumatra is called *Tanah* Jawa. PTOLEMY has both Jaba and Saba."—" Logan, Journ. Ind. Arch., iv, 338." In the Brunai use of the term, there is always some idea of a Northerly direction; for instance, I have heard a Brunai man who was passing from the South to the Northern side of his river, say he was going *Saba*. When the Company's Government was first inaugurated, the territory was, in official documents, mentioned as Sabah, a name which is still current amongst the natives, to whom the now officially accepted designation of *North Borneo* is meaningless and difficult of pronunciation.

Having settled with the Brunai authorities, Baron VON OVERBECK next proceeded to Sulu, and found the Sultan driven out of his capital, Sugh or Jolo, by the Spaniards, with whom he was still at war, and residing at Maibun, in the principal island of the Sulu Archipelago. After brief negotiations, the Sultan made to Baron VON OVERBECK and Mr. ALFRED DENT a grant of his rights and powers over the territories and lands tributary to him on the mainland of the island of Borneo, from the Pandassan River on the North West Coast to the Sibuko River on the East, and further invested the Baron, or his duly appointed successor in the office of supreme ruler of the Company's territories in Borneo, with the high sounding titles of Datu Bandahara and Raja of Sandakan.

On a company being formed to work the concessions, Baron VON OVERBECK resigned these titles from the Brunai and Sulu Potentates and they have not since been made use of, and the Baron himself terminated his connection with the country.

The grant from the Sultan of Sulu bears date the 22nd January, 1878, and on the 22nd July of the same year he signed a treaty, or act of re-submission to Spain. The Spanish Government claimed that, by previous treaties with Sulu, the suzerainty of Spain over Sulu and its dependencies in Borneo had been recognised and that consequently the grant to Mr. DENT was void. The British Government did not, however, fall in with this view, and in the early part of 1879, being then Acting Consul-General in Borneo, I was despatched to Sulu and to different points in North Borneo to publish, on behalf of our Government, a protest against the claim of Spain to any portion of the country. In March, 1885, a protocol was signed by which, in return for the recognition by England and Germany of Spanish sovereignty throughout the Archipelago of Sulu, Spain renounced all claims of sovereignty over territories on the Continent of Borneo which had belonged to the Sultan of Sulu, including the islands of Balambangan, Banguey and Malawali, as well as all those comprised within a zone of three maritime leagues from the coast.

Holland also strenuously objected to the cessions and to their recognition, on the ground that the general tenor of the Treaty of London of 1824 shews that a mixed occupation by England and the Netherlands of any island in the Indian Archipelago ought to be avoided.

It is impossible to discover anything in the treaty which bears out this contention. Borneo itself is not mentioned by name in the document, and the following clauses are the only ones regulating the future establishment of new Settlements in the Eastern Seas by either Power:—"Article 6. It is agreed that orders shall be given by the two Governments to their Officers and Agents in the East not to form any new Settlements on any of the islands in the Eastern Seas, without previous authority from their respective Governments in Europe. Art. 12. His Britannic Majesty, however, engages, that no British Establishment shall be made on the Carimon islands or on the islands of Battam, Bintang, Lingin, or on any of the other islands South of the Straits of Singapore, nor any treaty concluded by British authority with the chiefs of those islands." Without doubt, if Holland in 1824 had been desirous of prohibiting any British Settlement in the island of Borneo, such prohibition would have been expressed in this treaty. True, perhaps half of this great island is situated South of the Straits of Singapore, but the island cannot therefore be correctly said to lie to the South of the Straits and, at any rate, such a business-like nation as the Dutch would have noticed a weak point here and have included Borneo in the list with Battam and the other islands enumerated. Such was the view taken by Mr. GLADSTONE'S Cabinet, and Lord GRANVILLE informed the Dutch Minister in 1882 that the XIIth Article of the Treaty could not be taken to apply to Borneo, and "that as a a matter of international right they would have no ground to object even to the absolute annexation of North Borneo by Great Britain," and, moreover, as pointed out by his Lordship, the British had already a settlement in Borneo, namely the island of Labuan, ceded by the Sultan of Brunai in 1845 and confirmed by him in the Treaty of 1847. The case of Raja BROOKE in Sarawak was also practically that of a British Settlement in Borneo.

Lord GRANVILLE closed the discussion by stating that the grant of the Charter does not in any way imply the assumption of sovereign rights in North Borneo, *i.e.*, on the part of the British Government.

There the matter rested, but now that the Government is proposing* to include British North Borneo, Brunai and Sarawak under a formal "British Protectorate," the Netherlands Government is again raising objections, which they must be perfectly aware are groundless. It will be noted that the Dutch do not lay any claim to North Borneo themselves, having always recognized it as pertaining, with the Sulu Archipelago, to the Spanish Crown. It is only to the presence of the British Government in North Borneo that any objection is raised. In a "Resolution" of the Minister of State, Governor-General of Netherlands India, dated 28th February, 1846, occurs the following:—"The parts of Borneo on which the Netherlands does not exercise any influence are:—

   a. The States of the Sultan of Brunai or Borneo Proper;
      *   *   *   *   *

   b. The State of the Sultan of the Sulu Islands, having for boundaries on the West, the River Kimanis, the North and North-East Coasts as far as 3° N.L., where it is bounded by the River Atas, forming the extreme frontier towards the North with the State of Berow dependant on the Netherlands.

   c. All the islands of the Northern Coasts of Borneo."

Knowing this, Mr. ALFRED DENT put the limit of his cession from Sulu at the Sibuku River, the South bank of which is in N. Lat. 4° 5'; but towards the end of 1879, that is, long

---

* The Protectorate has since been proclaimed.

after the date of the cession, the Dutch hoisted their flag at Batu Tinagat in N. Lat. 4° 19′, thereby claiming the Sibuko and other rivers ceded by the Sultan of Sulu to the British Company. The dispute is still under consideration by our Foreign Office, but in September, 1883, in order to practically assert the Company's claims, I, as their Governor, had a very pleasant trip in a very small steam launch and steaming at full speed past two Dutch gun-boats at anchor, landed at the South bank of the Sibuko, temporarily hoisted the North Borneo flag, fired a *feu-de-joie*, blazed a tree, and returning, exchanged visits with the Dutch gun-boats, and entertained the Dutch Controlleur at dinner. Having carefully given the Commander of one of the gun-boats the exact bearings of the blazed tree, he proceeded in hot haste to the spot, and, I believe, exterminated the said tree. The Dutch Government complained of our having violated Netherlands territory, and matters then resumed their usual course, the Dutch station at Batu Tinagat, or rather at the Tawas River, being maintained unto this day.

As is hereafter explained, the cession of coast line from the Sultan of Brunai was not a continuous one, there being breaks on the West Coast in the case of a few rivers which were not included. The annual tribute to be paid to the Sultan was fixed at $12,000, and to the Pangeran Tumonggong $3,000—extravagantly large sums when it is considered that His Highness' revenue per annum from the larger portion of the territory ceded was *nil*. In March, 1881, through negotiations conducted by Mr. A. H. EVERETT, these sums were reduced to more reasonable proportions, namely, $5,000 in the case of the Sultan, and $2,500 in that of the Tumonggong.

The intermediate rivers which were not included in the Sultan's cession belonged to Chiefs of the blood royal, and the Sultan was unwilling to order them to be ceded, but in 1883 Resident DAVIES procured the cession from one of these Chiefs of the Pangalat River for an annual payment of $300, and subsequently the Putalan River was acquired for $1,000 per annum, and the Kawang River and the Mantanani Islands for lump sums of $1,300 and $350 respectively. In 1884, after prolonged negotiations, I was also enabled to obtain the cession of an important Province on the West Coast, to the South of the original boundary, to which the name of Dent Province has been given, and which includes the Padas and Kalias Rivers, and in the same deed of cession were also included two rivers which had been excepted in the first grant—the Tawaran and the Bangawan. The annual tribute under this cession is $3,100. The principal rivers within the Company's boundaries still unleased are the Kwala Lama, Membakut, Inanam and Menkabong. For fiscal reasons, and for the better prevention of the smuggling of arms and ammunition for sale to head-hunting tribes, it is very desirable that the Government of these remaining independent rivers should be acquired by the Company.

On the completion of the negotiations with the two Sultans, Baron VON OVERBECK, who was shortly afterwards joined by Mr. DENT, hoisted his flag—the house flag of Mr. DENT'S firm—at Sandakan, on the East Coast, and at Tampassuk and Pappar on the West, leaving at each a European, with a few so-called Police to represent the new Government, agents from the Sultans of Sulu and Brunai accompanying him to notify to the people that the supreme power had been transferred to Europeans. The common people heard the announcement with their usual apathy, but the officer left in charge had a difficult part to play with the headmen who, in the absence of any strong central Government, had practically usurped the functions of Government in many of the rivers. These Chiefs feared, and with reason, that not only would their importance vanish, but that trade with the inland tribes would be thrown open to all, and slave dealing be put a stop to under the new regime. At Sandakan, the Sultan's former Governor refused to recognise the changed position of affairs, but he had a resolute man to deal with in Mr. W. B. PRYER, and before he could do much harm, he lost his life by the capsizing of his prahu while on a trading voyage.

At Tampassuk, Mr. PRETYMAN, the Resident, had a very uncomfortable post, being in the midst of lawless, cattle-lifting and slave-dealing Bajaus and Illanuns. He, with the able assistance of Mr. F. X. WITTI, an ex-Naval officer of the

Austrian Service, who subsequently lost his life while exploring in the interior, and by balancing one tribe against another, managed to retain his position without coming to blows, and, on his relinquishing the service a few months afterwards, the arduous task of representing the Government without the command of any force to back up his authority developed on Mr. WITTI. In the case of the Pappar River, the former Chief, Datu BAHAR, declined to relinquish his position, and assumed a very defiant attitude. I was at that time in the Labuan service, and I remember proceeding to Pappar in an English man-of-war, in consequence of the disquieting rumours which had reached us, and finding the Resident, Mr. A. H. EVERETT, on one side of the small river with his house strongly blockaded and guns mounted in all available positions, and the Datu on the other side of the stream, immediately opposite to him, similarly armed to the teeth. But not a shot was fired, and Datu BAHAR is now a peaceable subject of the Company.

The most difficult problem, however, which these officers had to solve was that of keeping order, or trying to do so, amongst a lawless people, with whom for years past might had been right, and who considered kidnapping and cattle-lifting the occupations of honourable and high spirited gentlemen. That they effected what they did, that they kept the new flag flying and prepared the way for the Government of the Company, reflects the highest credit upon their pluck and diplomatic ingenuity, for they had neither police nor steam launches, nor the prestige which would have attached to them had they been representatives of the British Government, and under the well known British flag. They commenced their work with none of the *éclat* which surrounded Sir JAMES BROOKE in Sarawak, where he found the people in successful rebellion against the Sultan of Brunai, and was himself recognised as an agent of the British Government, so powerful that he could get the Queen's ships to attack the head hunting pirates, killing such numbers of them that, as I have said, the Head money claimed and awarded by the British Government reached the sum of £20,000. On the other hand, it is but fair to add that the fame of Sir JAMES' exploits and the action taken by Her Majesty's vessels, on his advice, in North-West Borneo years before, had inspired the natives with a feeling of respect for Englishmen which must have been a powerful factor in favour of the newly appointed officers. The native tribes, too, inhabiting North Borneo were more sub-divided, less warlike, and less powerful than those of Sarawak.

The promoters of the scheme were fortunate in obtaining the services, for the time being, as their chief representative in the East of Mr. W. H. READ, C.M.G., an old friend of Sir JAMES BROOKE, and who, as a Member of the Legislative Council of Singapore, and Consul-General for the Netherlands, had acquired an intimate knowledge of the Malay character and of the resources, capabilities and needs of Malayan countries.

On his return to England, Mr. DENT found that, owing to the opposition of the Dutch and Spanish Governments, and to the time required for a full consideration of the subject by Her Majesty's Ministers, there would be a considerable delay before a Royal Charter could be issued, meanwhile, the expenditure of the embryo Government in Borneo was not inconsiderable, and it was determined to form a "Provisional Association" to carry on till a Chartered Company could be formed.

Mr. DENT found an able supporter in Sir RUTHERFORD ALCOCK, K.C.B., who energetically advocated the scheme from patriotic motives, recognising the strategic and commercial advantages of the splendid harbours of North Borneo and the probability of the country becoming in the near future a not unimportant outlet for English commerce, now so heavily weighted by prohibitive tariffs in Europe and America.

The British North Borneo Provisional Association Limited, was formed in 1881, with a capital of £300,000, the Directors being Sir RUTHERFORD ALCOCK, Mr. A. DENT, Mr. R. B. MARTIN, Admiral MAYNE, and Mr. W. H. READ. The Association acquired from the original lessees the grants and commissions from the Sultans, with the object of disposing of these territories, lands and property to a Company to be incorporated by Royal Charter. This Charter passed the Great

Seal on the 1st November, 1881, and constituted and incorporated the gentlemen above-mentioned as "The British North Borneo Company."

The Provisional Association was dissolved, and the Chartered Company started on its career in May, 1882. The nominal capital was two million pounds, in £20 shares, but the number of shares issued, including 4,500 fully paid ones representing £90,000 to the vendors, was only 33,030, equal to £660,600, but on 23,449 of these shares only £12 have so far been called up. The actual cash, therefore, which the Company has had to work with and to carry on the development of the country from the point at which the original concessionaires and the Provisional Association had left it, is, including some £1,000 received for shares forfeited, about £384,000, and they have a right of call for £187,592 more. The Charter gave official recognition to the concessions from the Native Princes, conferred extensive powers on the Company as a corporate body, provided for the just government of the natives and for the gradual abolition of slavery, and reserved to the Crown the right of disapproving of the person selected by the Company to be their Governor in the East, and of controlling the Company's dealings with any Foreign Power.

The Charter also authorised the Company to use a distinctive flag, indicating the British character of the undertaking, and the one adopted, following the example of the English Colonies, is the British flag, "defaced," as it is termed, with the Company's badge—a lion. I have little doubt that this selection of the British flag, in lieu of the one originally made use of, had a considerable effect in imbuing the natives with an idea of the stability and permanence of the Company's Government.

Mr. DENT'S house flag was unknown to them before and, on the West Coast, many thought that the Company's presence in the country might be only a brief one, like that of its predecessor, the American syndicate, and, consequently, were afraid to tender their allegiance, since, on the Company's withdrawal, they would be left to the tender mercies of their former Chiefs. But the British flag was well-known to those of them who were traders, and they had seen it flying for many a year in the Colony of Labuan and on board the vessels which had punished their piratical acts in former days.

Then, too, I was soon able to organise a Police Force mainly composed of Sikhs, and was provided with a couple of steam-launches. Owing doubtless to that and other causes, the refractory chiefs, soon after the Company's formation, appeared to recognize that the game of opposition to the new order of things was a hopeless one.

Chapter VIII.

The area of the territory ceded by the original grants was estimated at 20,000 square miles, but the additions which have been already mentioned now bring it up to about 31,000 square miles, including adjacent islands, so that it is somewhat larger than Ceylon, which is credited with only 25,365 square miles. In range of latitude, in temperature and in rainfall, North Borneo presents many points of resemblance to Ceylon, and it was at first thought that it might be possible to attract to the new country some of the surplus capital, energy and aptitude for planting which had been the foundation of Ceylon's prosperity.

Even the expression "The New Ceylon" was employed as an alternative designation for the country, and a description of it under that title was published by the well known writer— Mr. JOSEPH HATTON.

These hopes have not so far been realized, but on the other hand North Borneo is rapidly becoming a second Sumatra, Dutchmen, Germans and some English having discovered the suitability of its soil and climate for producing tobacco of a quality fully equal to the famed Deli leaf of that island.

The coast line of the territory is about one thousand miles, and a glance at the map will shew that it is furnished with capital harbours, of which the principal are Gaya Bay on the West, Kudat in Marudu Bay on the North, and Sandakan Harbour on the East. There are several others, but at those enumerated the Company have opened their principal stations.

Of the three mentioned, the more striking is that of Sandakan, which is 15 miles in length, with a width varying from 1¼ miles, at its entrance, to 5 miles at the broadest part. It is here that the present capital is situated—Sandakan, a town containing a population of not more than 5,000 people, of whom perhaps thirty are Europeans and a thousand Chinese. For its age, Sandakan has suffered serious vicissitudes. It was founded by Mr. PRYER, in 1878, well up the bay, but was soon afterwards burnt to the ground. It was then transferred to its present position, nearer the mouth of the harbour, but in May, 1886, the whole of what was known as the "Old Town" was utterly consumed by fire; in about a couple of hours there being nothing left of the *atap*-built shops and houses but the charred piles and posts on which they had been raised above the ground. When a fire has once laid hold of an atap town, probably no exertions would much avail to check it; certainly our Chinese held this opinion, and it was impossible to get them to move hand or foot in assisting the Europeans and Police in their efforts to confine its ravages to as limited an area as possible. They entertain the idea that such futile efforts tend only to aggravate the evil spirits and increase their fury. The Hindu shopkeepers were successful in saving their quarter of the town by means of looking glasses, long prayers and chants. It is now forbidden to any one to erect atap houses in the town, except in one specified area to which such structures are confined. Most of the present houses are of plank, with tile, or corrugated iron roofs, and the majority of the shops are built over the sea, on substantial wooden piles, some of the principal "streets," including that to which the ambitious name of "The Praya" has been given, being similarly constructed on piles raised three or four feet above high water mark. The reason is that, owing to the steep hills at the back of the site, there is little available flat land for building on, and, moreover, the pushing Chinese trader always likes to get his shops as near as possible to the sea—the highway of the "prahus" which bring him the products of the neighbouring rivers and islands. In time, no doubt, the Sandakan hills will be used to reclaim more land from the sea, and the town will cease to be an amphibious one. In the East there are, from a sanitary point of view, some points of advantage in having a tide-way passing under the houses. I should add that Sandakan is a creation of the Company's and not a native town taken over by them. When Mr. PRYER first hoisted his flag, there was only one solitary Chinaman and no Europeans in the harbour, though at one time, during the Spanish blockade of Sulu, a Singapore firm had established a trading station, known as "Kampong German," using it as their head-quarters from which to run the blockade of Sulu, which they successfully did for some considerable time, to their no small gain and advantage. The success attending the Germans' venture excited the emulation of the Chinese traders of Labuan, who found their valuable Sulu trade cut off and, through the good offices of the Government of the Colony, they were enabled to charter the Sultan of Brunai's smart little yacht the *Sultana*, and engaging the services as Captain of an ex-member of the Labuan Legislative Council, they endeavoured to enact the roll of blockade runner. After a trip or two, however, the *Sultana* was taken by the Spaniards, snugly at anchor in a Sulu harbour, the Captain and Crew having time to make their escape. As she was not under the British flag, the poor Sultan could obtain no redress, although the blockade was not recognised as effective by the European Powers and English and German vessels, similarly seized, had been restored to their owners. The *Sultana* proved a convenient despatch boat for the Spanish authories. The Sultan of Sulu to prove his friendship to the Labuan traders, had an unfortunate man cut to pieces with krisses, on the charge of having betrayed the vessel's position to the blockading cruisers.

Sandakan is one of the few places in Borneo which has been opened and settled without much fever and sickness ensuing, and this was due chiefly to the soil being poor and sandy and to there being an abundance of good, fresh, spring water. It may be stated, as a general rule, that the richer the soil the more deadly will be the fever the pioneers will have to encounter when the primeval jungle is first felled and the sun's rays admitted to the virgin soil.

Sandakan is the principal trading station in the Company's territory, but with Hongkong only 1,200 miles distant in one direction, Manila 600 miles in another, and Singapore 1,000 miles in a third, North Borneo can never become an emporium for the trade of the surrounding countries and islands, and the Court of Directors must rest content with developing their own local trade and pushing forward, by wise and encouraging regulations, the planting interest, which seems to have already taken firm root in the country and which will prove to be the foundation of its future prosperity. Gold and other minerals, including coal, are known to exist, but the mineralogical exploration of a country covered with forest and destitute of roads is a work requiring time, and we are not yet in a position to pronounce on North Borneo's expectations in regard to its mineral wealth.

The gold on the Segama River, on the East coast, has been several times reported on, and has been proved to exist in sufficient quantities to, at any rate, well repay the labours of Chinese gold diggers, but the district is difficult of access by water, and the Chinese are deferring operations on a large scale until the Government has constructed a road into the district. A European Company has obtained mineral concessions on the river, but has not yet decided on its mode of operation, and individual European diggers have tried their luck on the fields, hitherto without meeting with much success, owing to heavy rains, sickness and the difficulty of getting up stores. The Company will probably find that Chinese diggers will not only stand the climate better, but will be more easily governed, be satisfied with smaller returns, and contribute as much or more than the Europeans to the Government Treasury, by their consumption of opium, tobacco and other excisable articles, by fees for gold licenses, and so forth.

Another source of natural wealth lies in the virgin forest with which the greater portion of the country is clothed, down to the water's edge. Many of the trees are valuable as timber, especially the *Billian*, or Borneo iron-wood tree, which is impervious to the attacks of white-ants ashore and almost equally so to those of the *teredo navalis* afloat, and is wonderfully enduring of exposure to the tropical sun and the tropical downpours of rain. I do not remember having ever come across a bit of *billian* that showed signs of decay during a residence of seventeen years in the East. The wood is very heavy and sinks in water, so that, in order to be shipped, it has to be floated on rafts of soft wood, of which there is an abundance of excellent quality, of which one kind—the red *serayah*—is likely to come into demand by builders in England. Other of the woods, such as *mirabau, penagah* and *rengas*, have good grain and take a fine polish, causing them to be suitable for the manufacture of furniture. The large tree which yields the Camphor *barus* of commerce also affords good timber. It is a *Dryobalanops,* and is not to be confused with the *Cinnamomum camphora*, from which the ordinary "camphor" is obtained and the wood of which retains the camphor smell and is largely used by the Chinese in the manufacture of boxes, the scented wood keeping off ants and other insects which are a pest in the Far East. The Borneo camphor tree is found only in Borneo and Sumatra. The camphor which is collected for export, principally to China and India, by the natives, is found in a solid state in the trunk, but only in a small percentage of the trees, which are felled by the collectors. The price of this camphor *barus* as it is termed, is said to be nearly a hundred times as much as that of the ordinary camphor, and it is used by the Chinese and Indians principally for embalming purposes. Billian and other woods enumerated are all found near the coast and, generally, in convenient proximity to some stream, and so easily available for export. Sandakan harbour has some thirteen rivers and streams running into it, and, as the native population is very small, the jungle has been scarcely touched, and no better locality could, therefore, be desired by a timber merchant. Two European Timber Companies are now doing a good business there, and the Chinese also take their share of the trade. China affords a ready and large market for Borneo timber, being itself almost forestless, and for many years past it has received ironwood from Sarawak. Borneo timber has also been exported to the Straits Settlements, Australia and Mauritius, and I hear that an order has been given for England. Iron wood is only found in certain districts, notably in Sandakan Bay and on the East coast, being rarely met with on the West coast. I have seen a private letter from an officer in command of a British man-of-war who had some samples of it on board which came in very usefully when certain bearings of the screw shaft were giving out on a long voyage, and were found to last *three times* as long as lignum vitæ.

In process of time, as the country is opened up by roads and railways, doubtless many other valuable kinds of timber trees will be brought to light in the interior.

A notice of Borneo Forests would be incomplete without a reference to the mangroves, which are such a prominent feature of the country as one approaches it by sea, lining much of the coast and forming, for mile after mile, the actual banks of most of the rivers. Its thick, dark-green, never changing foliage helps to give the new comer that general impression of dull monotony in tropical scenery, which, perhaps, no one, except the professed botanist, whose trained and practical eye never misses the smallest detail, ever quite shakes off.

The wood of the mangrove forms most excellent firewood, and is often used by small steamers as an economical fuel in lieu of coal, and is exported to China in the timber ships. The bark is also a separate article of export, being used as a dye and for tanning, and is said to contain nearly 42% of *tannin*.

The value of the general exports from the territory is increasing every year, having been $145,444 in 1881 and $525,879 in 1888. With the exception of tobacco and pepper, the list is almost entirely made up of the natural raw products of the land and sea—such as bees'-wax, camphor, damar, gutta percha, the sap of a large forest tree destroyed in the process of collection of gutta, India rubber, from a creeper likewise destroyed by the collectors, rattans, well known to every school boy, sago, timber, edible birds'-nests, seed-pearls, Mother-o'-pearl shells in small quantities, dried fish and dried sharks'-fins, trepang (sea-slug or bêche-de-mer), aga, or edible sea-weed, tobacco (both Native and European grown), pepper, and occasionally elephants' tusks—a list which shews the country to be a rich store house of natural productions, and one which will be added to, as the land is brought under cultivation with coffee, tea, sugar, cocoa, Manila hemp, pine apple fibre, and other tropical products for which the soil, and especially the rainfall, temperature and climatic conditions generally, including entire freedom from typhoons and earthquakes, eminently adapt it, and many of which have already been tried with success on an experimental scale. As regards pepper, it has been previously shewn that North Borneo was in former days an exporter of this spice. Sugar has been grown by the natives for their own consumption for many years, as also tapioca, rice and Indian corn. It is not my object to give a detailed list of the productions of the country, and I would refer any reader who is anxious to be further enlightened on these and kindred topics to the excellent "Hand-book of British North Borneo," prepared for the Colonial and Indian Exhibition of 1886, at which the new Colony was represented, and published by Messrs. WILLIAM CLOWES & SONS.

The edible birds'-nests are already a source of considerable revenue to the Government, who let out the collection of them for annual payments, and also levy an export duty as they leave the country for China, which is their only market. The nests are about the size of those of the ordinary swallow and are formed by innumerable hosts of swifts—*Collocalia fuciphaga*—entirely from a secretion of the glands of the throat. These swifts build in caves, some of which are of very large dimensions, and there are known to be some sixteen of them in different parts of British North Borneo. With only one exception, the caves occur in limestone rocks and, generally, at no great distance from the sea, though some have been discovered in the interior, on the banks of the Kinabatangan River. The exception above referred to is that of a small cave on a sand-stone island at the entrance of Sandakan harbour. The *Collocalia fuciphaga* appears to be pretty well distributed over the Malayan islands, but of these, Borneo and Java are the principal sources of supply. Nests are also exported from the Andaman Islands, and a revenue of £30,000 a year is said to be derived from the nests in the small islands in the inland sea of Tab Sab, inhabited by natives of Malay stock.

The finest caves, or rather series of caves, as yet known in the Company's territories are those of Gomanton, a limestone hill situated at the head of the Sapa Gaia, one of the streams running into Sandakan harbour.

These grand caves, which are one of the most interesting sights in the country, are, in fine weather, easily accessible from the town of Sandakan, by a water journey across the harbour and up the Sapa Gaia, of about twelve miles, and by a road from the point of debarkation to the entrance of the lower caves, about eight miles in length.

The height of the hill is estimated at 1,000 feet, and it contains two distinct series of caves. The first series is on the "ground floor" and is known as *Simud Hitam*, or "black entrance." The magnificent porch, 250 feet high and 100 broad, which gives admittance to this series, is on a level with the river bank, and, on entering, you find yourself in a spacious and lofty chamber well lighted from above by a large open space, through which can be seen the entrance to the upper set of caves, some 400 to 500 feet up the hill side. In this chamber is a large deposit of guano, formed principally by the myriads of bats inhabiting the caves in joint occupancy with the edible-nest-forming swifts. Passing through this first chamber and turning a little to the right you come to a porch leading into an extensive cave, which extends under the upper series. This cave is filled half way up to its roof, with an enormous deposit of guano, which has been estimated to be 40 to 50 feet in depth. How far the cave extends has not been ascertained, as its exploration, until some of the deposit is removed, would not be an easy task, for the explorer would be compelled to walk along on the top of the guano, which in some places is so soft that you sink in it almost up to your waist. My friend Mr. C. A. BAMPFYLDE, in whose company I first visited Gomanton, and who, as "Commissioner of Birds-nest Caves," drew up a very interesting report on them, informed me that, though he had found it impossible to explore right to the end, he had been a long way in and was confident that the cave was of very large size. To reach the upper series of caves, you leave Simud Hitam and clamber up the hill side—a steep but not difficult climb, as the jagged limestone affords sure footing. The entrance to this series, known as *Simud Putih*, or "white entrance," is estimated to be at an elevation of 300 feet above sea level, and the porch by which you enter them is about 30 feet high by about 50 wide. The floor slopes steeply downwards and brings you into an enormous cave, with smaller ones leading off it, all known to the nest collectors by their different native names. You soon come to a large black hole, which has never been explored, but which is said to communicate with the large guano cave below, which has been already described. Passing on, you enter a dome-like cave, the height of the roof or ceiling of which has been estimated at 800 feet, but for the accuracy of this guess I cannot vouch. The average height of the cave before the domed portion is reached is supposed to be about 150 feet, and Mr. BAMPFYLDE estimates the total length, from the entrance to the furthest point, at a fifth of a mile. The Simud Putih series are badly lighted, there being only a few "holes" in the roof of the dome, so that torches or lights of some kind are required. There are large deposits of guano in these caves also, which could be easily worked by lowering quantities down into the Simud Hitam caves below, the floor of which, as already stated, is on a level with the river bank, so that a tramway could be laid right into them and the guano be carried down to the port of shipment, at the mouth of the Sapa Gaia River. Samples of the guano have been sent home, and have been analysed by Messrs. VOELCKER & CO. It is rich in ammonia and nitrogen and has been valued at £5 to £7 a ton in England. The bat-guano is said to be richer as a manure than that derived from the swifts. To ascend to the top of Gomanton, one has to emerge from the Simud Putih entrance and, by means of a ladder, reach an overhanging ledge, whence a not very difficult climb brings one to the cleared summit, from which a fine view of the surrounding country is obtained, including Kina-balu, the sacred mountain of North Borneo. On this summit will be found the holes already described as helping to somewhat lighten the darkness of the dome-shaped cave, on the roof of which we are in fact now standing. It is through these holes that the natives lower themselves into the caves, by means of rattan ladders and, in a most marvellous manner, gain a footing on the ceiling and construct cane stages, by means of which they can reach any part of the roof and, either by hand or by a suitable pole to the end of which is attached a lighted candle, secure the wealth-giving luxury for the epicures of China. There are two principal seasons for collecting the nests, and care has to be taken that the collection is made punctually at the proper time, before the eggs are all hatched, otherwise the nests become dirty and fouled with feathers, &c., and discoloured and injured by the damp, thereby losing much of their market value. Again, if the nests are not collected for a season, the birds do not build many new ones in the following season, but make use of the old ones, which thereby become comparatively valueless.

There are, roughly speaking, three qualities of nests, sufficiently described by their names—white, red, and black—the best quality of each fetching, at Sandakan, per catty of 1⅓ lbs., $16, $7 and 8 cents respectively.

The question as to the true cause of the difference in the nests has not yet been satisfactorily solved. Some allege that the red and black nests are simply white ones deteriorated by not having been collected in due season. I myself incline to agree with the natives that the nests are formed by different birds, for the fact that, in one set of caves, black nests are always found together in one part, and white ones in another, though both are collected with equal care and punctuality, seems almost inexplicable under the first theory. It is true that the different kinds of nests are not found in the same season, and it is just possible that the red and black nests may be the second efforts at building made by the swifts after the collectors have disturbed them by gathering their first, white ones. In the inferior nests, feathers are found *mixed up* with the gelatinous matter forming the walls, as though the glands were unable to secrete a sufficient quantity of material, and the bird had to eke it out with its own feathers. In the substance of the white nests no feathers are found.

Then, again, it is sometimes found in the case of two distinct caves, situated at no great distance apart, that the one yields almost entirely white nests, and the other nearly all red, or black ones, though the collections are made with equal regularity in each. The natives, as I have said, seem to think that there are two kinds of birds, and the Hon. R. ABER-

CROMBY reports that, when he visited Gomanton, they shewed him eggs of different size and explained that one was laid by the white-nest bird and the other by the black-nest builder. Sir HUGH LOW, in his work on Sarawak, published in 1848, asserts that there are "two different and quite dissimilar kinds of birds, though both are swallows" (he should have said swifts), and that the one which produces the white nest is larger and of more lively colours, with a white belly, and is found on the sea-coast, while the other is smaller and darker and found more in the interior. He admits, however, that though he had opportunities of observing the former, he had not been able to procure a specimen.

The question is one which should be easily settled on the spot, and I recommend it to the consideration of the authorities of the British North Borneo Museum, which has been established at Sandakan.

The annual value of the nests of Gomanton, when properly collected, has been reckoned at \$23,000, but I consider this an excessive estimate. My friend Mr. A. COOK, the Treasurer of the Territory, to whose zeal and perseverance the Company owes much, has arranged with the Buludupih tribe to collect these nests on payment to the Government of a royalty of \$7,500 per annum, which is in addition to the export duty at the rate of 10% *ad valorem* paid by the Chinese exporters.

The swifts and bats—the latter about the size of the ordinary English bat—avail themselves of the shelter afforded by the caves without incommoding one another, for, by a sort of Box and Cox arrangement, the former occupy the caves during the night and the latter by day.

Standing at the Simud Putih entrance about 5 P. M., the visitor will suddenly hear a whirring sound from below, which is caused by the myriads of bats issuing, for their nocturnal banquet, from the Simud Itam caves, through the wide open space that has been described. They come out in a regularly ascending continuous spiral or corkscrew coil, revolving from left to right in a very rapid and regular manner. When the top of the spiral coil reaches a certain height, a colony of bats breaks off, and continuing to revolve in a well kept ring from left to right gradually ascends higher and higher, until all of a sudden the whole detachment dashes off in the direction of the sea, towards the mangrove swamps and the *nipas*. Sometimes these detached colonies reverse the direction of their revolutions after leaving the main body, and, instead of from left to right, revolve from right to left. Some of them continue for a long time revolving in a circle, and attain a great height before darting off in quest of food, while others make up their minds more expeditiously, after a few revolutions. Amongst the bats, three white ones were, on the occasion of my visit, very conspicuous, and our followers styled them the Raja, his wife and child. Hawks and sea-eagles are quickly attracted to the spot, but only hover on the outskirts of the revolving coil, occasionally snapping up a prize. I also noticed several hornbills, but they appeared to have been only attracted by curiosity. Mr. BAMPFYLDE informed me that, on a previous visit, he had seen a large green snake settled on an overhanging branch near which the bats passed and that occasionally he managed to secure a victim. I timed the bats and found that they took almost exactly fifty minutes to come out of the caves, a thick stream of them issuing all that time and at a great pace, and the reader can endeavour to form for himself some idea of their vast numbers. They had all got out by ten minutes to six in the evening, and at about six o'clock the swifts began to come home to roost. They came in in detached, independent parties, and I found it impossible to time them, as some of them kept very late hours. I slept in the Simud Putih cave on this occasion, and found hat next morning the bats returned about 5 A.M., and that he swifts went out an hour afterwards.

As shewing the mode of formation of these caves, I may add that I noticed, imbedded in a boulder of rock in the upper caves, two pieces of coral and several fossil marine shells, bivalves and others.

The noise made by the bats going out for their evening promenade resembled a combination of that of the surf breaking on a distant shore and of steam being gently blown off from a vessel which has just come to anchor.

There are other interesting series of caves, and one—that of Madai, in Darvel Bay on the East coast—was

BRITISH BORNEO.

visited by the late Lady BRASSEY and Miss BRASSEY in April, 1887, when British North Borneo was honoured by a visit of the celebrated yacht the *Sunbeam*, with Lord BRASSEY and his family on board.

I accompanied the party on the trip to Madai, and shall not easily forget the pluck and energy with which Lady BRASSEY, then in bad health, surmounted the difficulties of the jungle track, and insisted upon seeing all that was to be seen; or the gallant style in which Miss BRASSEY unwearied after her long tramp through the forest, led the way over the slippery boulders in the dark caves.

The Chinese ascribe great strengthening powers to the soup made of the birds'-nests, which they boil down into a syrup with barley sugar, and sip out of tea cups. The gelatinous looking material of which the substance of the nests is composed is in itself almost flavourless.

It is also with the object of increasing their bodily powers that these epicures consume the uninviting sea-slug or bêche-de-mer, and dried sharks'-fins and cuttle fish.

To conclude my brief sketch of Sandakan Harbour and of the Capital, it should be stated that, in addition to being within easy distance of Hongkong, it lies but little off the usual route of vessels proceeding from China to Australian ports, and can be reached by half a day's deviation of the ordinary track.

Should, unfortunately, war arise with Russia, there is little doubt their East Asiatic squadron would endeavour both to harass the Australian trade and to damage, as much as possible, the coast towns, in which case the advantages of Sandakan, midway between China and Australia, as a base of operations for the British protecting fleet would at once become manifest. It is somewhat unfortunate that a bar has formed just outside the entrance of the harbour, with a depth of water of four fathoms at low water, spring tides, so that ironclads of the largest size would be denied admittance.

There are at present, no steamers sailing direct from Borneo to England, and nearly all the commerce from British North Borneo ports is carried by local steamers to that great emporium of the trade of the Malayan countries, Singapore, distant from Sandakan a thousand miles, and it is a curious fact, that though many of the exports are ultimately intended for the China market, *e.g.*, edible birds'-nests, the Chinese traders find it pays them better to send their produce to Singapore in the first instance, instead of direct to Hongkong. This is partly accounted for by the further fact that, though the Government has spent considerable sum in endeavouring to attract Chinamen from China, the large proportion of our Chinese traders and of the Chinese population generally has come to us *viâ* Singapore, after as it were having undergone there an education in the knowledge of Malayan affairs.

As further illustrating the commercial and strategical advantages of the harbours of British North Borneo, it should be noted that the course recommended by the Admiralty instructions for vessels proceeding to China from the Straits, *viâ* the Palawan passage, brings them within ninety miles of the harbours of the West Coast.

As to postal matters, British North Borneo, though not in the Postal Union, has entered into arrangements for the exchange of direct closed mails with the English Post Office, London, with which latter also, as well as with Singapore and India, a system of Parcel Post and of Post Office Orders has been established.

The postal and inland revenue stamps, distinguished by the lion, which has been adopted as the Company's badge, are well executed and in considerable demand with stamp collectors, owing to their rarity.

The Government also issues its own copper coinage, one cent and half-cent pieces, manufactured in Birmingham and of the same intrinsic value as those of Hongkong and the Straits Settlements.

The revenue derived from its issue is an important item to the Colony's finances, and considerable quantities have been put ino circulation, not only within the limits of the Company's territory, but also in Brunai and in the British Colony of Labuan, where it has been proclaimed a legal tender on the condition of the Company, in return for the profit which they reap by its issue in the island, contributing to the impoverished Colonial Treasury the yearly sum of $3,000.

Trade, however, is still, to a great extent, carried on by a system of barter with the Natives. The primitive currency medium in vogue under the native regime has been described in the Chapters on Brunai.

The silver currency is the Mexican and Spanish Dollar and the Japanese Yen, supplemented by the small silver coinage of the Straits Settlements. The Company has not yet minted any silver coinage, as the profit thereon is small, but in the absence of a bank, the Treasury, for the convenience of traders and planters, carries on banking business to a certain extent, and issues bank notes of the values of $1, $5 and $25, cash reserves equal to one-third of the value of the notes in circulation being maintained.*

Sir ALFRED DENT is taking steps to form a Banking Company at Sandakan, the establishment of which would materially assist in the development of the resources of the territory.

British North Borneo is not in telegraphic communication with any part of the world, except of course through Singapore, nor are there any local telegraphs. The question, however, of supplementing the existing cable between the Straits Settlements and China by another touching at British territory in Borneo has more than once been mooted, and may yet become a *fait accompli*. The Spanish Government appear to have decided to unite Sulu by telegraphic communication with the rest of the world, *via* Manila, and this will bring Sandakan within 180 miles of the telegraphic station.

CHAPTER IX.

In the eyes of the European planter, British North Borneo is chiefly interesting as a field for the cultivation of tobacco, in rivalry to Sumatra, and my readers may judge of the importance of this question from a glance at the following figures, which shew the dividends declared of late years by three of the principal Tobacco Planting Companies in the latter island :—

---

* Agencies of Singapore Banks have since been established at Sandakan.

	Dividends paid by		
In	The Deli Maatschappi.	The Tabak Maatschappi.	The Amsterdam Deli Co.
1882	65 per cent. ...	25 per cent. ...	10 per cent.
1883	101 ,, ...	50 ,, ...	30 ,,
1884	77 ,, ...	60 ,, ...	30 ,,
1885	107 ,, ...	100 ,, ...	60 ,,
1886	108 ,, ...		

In Sumatra, under Dutch rule, tobacco culture can at present only be carried on in certain districts, where the soil is suitable and where the natives are not hostile, and, as most of the best land has been taken up, and planters are beginning to feel harassed by the stringent regulations and heavy taxation of the Dutch Government, both Dutch and German planters are turning their attention to British North Borneo, where they find the regulations easier, and the authorities most anxious to welcome them, while, owing to the scanty population, there is plenty of available land. It is but fair to say that the first experiment in North Borneo was made by an English, or rather an Anglo-Chinese Company, the China-Sabah Land Farming Company, who, on hurriedly selected land in Sandakan and under the disadvantages which usually attend pioneers in a new country, shipped a crop to England which was pronounced by experts in 1886 to equal in quality the best Sumatra-grown leaf. Unfortunately, this Company, which had wasted its resources on various experiments, instead of confining itself to tobacco planting, was unable to continue its operations, but a Dutch planter from Java, Count GELOES D'ELSLOO, having carefully selected his land in Marudu Bay, obtained, in 1887, the high average of $1 per lb. for his trial crop at Amsterdam, and, having formed an influential Company in Europe, is energetically bringing a large area under cultivation, and has informed me that he confidently expects to rival Sumatra, not only in quality, but also in quantity of leaf per acre, as some of his men have cut twelve pikuls per field, whereas six pikuls per field is usually considered a good crop. The question of "quantity" is a very important one, for quality without quantity will never pay on a tobacco estate. Several Dutchmen have followed Count GELOES' example, and two German Companies and one British are now at work in the country. Altogether, fully 350,000 acres* of land have been taken up for tobacco cultivation in British North Borneo up to the present time.

In selecting land for this crop, climate, that is, temperature and rainfall, has equally to be considered with richness of soil. For example, the soil of Java is as rich, or richer than that of Sumatra, but owing to its much smaller rainfall, the tobacco it produces commands nothing like the prices fetched by that of the former. The seasons and rainfall in Borneo are found to be very similar to those of Sumatra. The average recorded annual rainfall at Sandakan for the last seven years is given by Dr. WALKER, the Principal Medical Officer, as 124.34 inches, the range being from 156.9 to 101.26 inches per annum.

Being so near the equator, roughly speaking between N. Latitudes 4 and 7, North Borneo has, unfortunately for the European residents whose lot is cast there, nothing that can be called a winter, the temperature remaining much about the same from year's end to year's end. It used to seem to me that during the day the thermometer was generally about 83 or 85 in the shade, but, I believe, taking the year all round, night and day, the mean temperature is 81, and the extremes recorded on the coast line are 67.5 and 94.5. Dr. WALKER has not yet extended his stations to the hills in the interior, but mentions it as probable that freezing point is occasionally reached near the top of the Kinabalu Mountains, which is 13,700 feet high; he adds that the lowest recorded temperature he has found is 36.5, given by Sir SPENCER ST. JOHN in his "Life in the Forests of the Far East." Snow has never

---

* Governor CREAGH tells me 600,000 acres have now been taken up.

been reported even on Kinabalu, and I am informed that the Charles Louis Mountains in Dutch New Guinea, are the only ones in tropical Asia where the limit of perpetual snow is attained. I must stop to say a word in praise of Kinabalu, "the Chinese Widow,"* the sacred mountain of North Borneo whither the souls of the righteous Dusuns ascend after death. It can be seen from both coasts, and appears to rear its isolated, solid bulk almost straight out of the level country, so dwarfed are the neighbouring hills by its height of 13,680 feet. The best view of it is obtained, either at sunrise or at sunset, from the deck of a ship proceeding along the West Coast, from which it is about twenty miles inland. During the day time the Widow, as a rule, modestly veils her features in the clouds.

The effect when its huge mass is lighted up at evening by the last rays of the setting sun is truly magnificent.

On the spurs of Kinabalu and on the other lofty hills, of which there is an abundance, no doubt, as the country becomes opened up by roads many suitable sites for sanitoria will be discovered, and the day will come when these hill sides, like those of Ceylon and Java, will be covered with thriving plantations.

Failing winter, the Bornean has to be content with the the change afforded by a dry and a wet season, the latter being looked upon as the "winter," and prevailing during the month of November, December and January. But though the two seasons are sufficiently well defined and to be depended upon by planters, yet there is never a month during the dry season when no rain falls, nor in the wet season are fine days at all rare The dryest months appear to be March and April, and in June there generally occurs what Doctor WALKER terms an "intermediate" and moderately wet period.

Tobacco is a crop which yields quick returns, for in about 110 to 120 days after the seed is sown the plant is ripe for cutting. The *modus operandi* is somewhat after this fashion. First select your land, virgin soil covered with untouched

---

* For the native derivation of this appellation see page 54.

jungle, situated at a distance from the sea, so that no salt breezes may jeopardise the proper burning qualities of the future crop, and as devoid as possible of hills. Then, a point of primary importance which will be again referred to, engage your Chinese coolies, who have to sign agreements for fixed periods, and to be carefully watched afterwards, as it is the custom to give them cash advances on signing, the repayment of which they frequently endeavour to avoid by slipping away just before your vessel sails and probably engaging themselves to another master.

Without the Chinese cooly, the tobacco planter is helpless, and if the proper season is allowed to pass, a whole year may be lost. The Chinaman is too expensive a machine to be employed on felling the forest, and for this purpose, indeed, the Malay is more suitable and the work is accordingly given him to do under contract. Simultaneously with the felling, a track should be cut right through the heart of the estate by the natives, to be afterwards ditched and drained and made passable for carts by the Chinese coolies.

That as much as possible of the felled jungle should be burned up is so important a matter and one that so greatly affects the individual Chinese labourer, that it is not left to the Malays to do, but, on the completion of the felling, the whole area which is to be planted is divided out into "fields," of about one acre each, and each "field" is assigned by lot to a Chinese cooly, whose duty it is to carefully burn the timber and plant, tend and finally cut the tobacco on his own division, for which he is remunerated in accordance with the quality and quantity of the leaf he is able to bring into the drying sheds. Each "field," having been cleared as carefully as may be of the felled timber, is next thoroughly hoed up, and a small "nursery" prepared in which the seeds provided by the manager are planted and protected from rain and sun by palm leaf mats (*kajangs*) raised on sticks. In about a week, the young plants appear, and the Chinese tenant, as I may call him, has to carefully water them morning and evening. As the young seedlings grow up, their enemy, the worms and grubs, find them out and attack them in such numbers that at least once a day, sometimes oftener, the anxious planter has to go through his nursery and pick them off, otherwise in a short time he would have no tobacco to plant out. About thirty days after the seed has been sown, the seedlings are old enough to be planted out in the field, which has been all the time carefully prepared for their reception. The first thing to be done is to make holes in the soil, at distances of two feet one way and three feet the other, the earth in them being loosened and broken up so that the tender roots should meet with no obstacles to their growth. As the holes are ready for them, the seedlings are taken from the nursery and planted out, being protected from the sun's rays either by fern, or coarse grass, or, in the best managed estates, by a piece of wood, like a roofing shingle, inserted in the soil in such a way as to provide the required shelter. The watering has to be continued till the plants have struck root, when the protecting shelter is removed and the earth banked up round them, care being taken to daily inspect them and remove the worms which have followed them from the nursery. The next operation is that of "topping" the plants, that is, of stopping their further growth by nipping off the heads.

According to the richness of the soil and the general appearance of the plants, this is ordered to be done by the European overseer after a certain number of leaves have been produced. If the soil is poor, perhaps only fourteen leaves will be allowed, while on the richest land the plant can stand and properly ripen as many as twenty-four leaves. The signs of ripening, which generally takes place in about three months from the date of transplantation, are well known to the overseers and are first shewn by a yellow tinge becoming apparent at the tips of the leaves.

The cooly thereupon cuts the plants down close to the ground and lightly and carefully packs them into long baskets so as not to injure the leaves, and carries them to the drying sheds. There they are examined by the overseer of his division, who credits him with the value, based on the quantity and quality of the crop he brings in, the price ranging from $1 up to $8 per thousand trees. The plants are then tied in rows on sticks, heads downwards, and hoisted up in tiers to dry in the shed.

After hanging for a fortnight, they are sufficiently dry and, being lowered down, are stripped of their leaves, which are tied up into small bundles, similar leaves being roughly sorted together.

The bundles of leaves are then taken to other sheds, where the very important process of fermenting them is carried out. For this purpose, they are put into orderly arranged heaps—small at first, but increased in size till very little heat is given out, the heat being tested by a thermometer, or even an ordinary piece of stick inserted into them. When the fermentation is nearly completed and the leaves have attained a fixed colour, they are carefully sorted according to colour, spottiness and freedom from injury of any kind. The price realized in Europe is greatly affected by the care with which the leaves have been fermented and sorted. Spottiness is not always considered a defect, as it is caused by the sun shining on the leaves when they have drops of rain on them, and to this the best leaves are liable; but spotted leaves, broken leaves and in short leaves having the same characteristics should be carefully sorted together. After this sorting is completed as regards class and quality, there is a further sorting in regard to length, and the leaves are then tied together in bundles of thirty-five. These bundles are put into large heaps and, when no more heating is apparent, they are ready to be pressed under a strong screw press and sewn up in bags which are carefully marked and shipped off to Europe—to Amsterdam as a rule.

As the coolies' payment is by "results," it is their interest to take the greatest care of their crops; but for any outside work they may be called on to perform, and for their services as sorters, etc. in the sheds, they are paid extra. During the whole time, also, they receive, for "subsistence" money, $4 or $3 a month. At the end of the season their accounts are made up, being debited with the amount of the original advance, subsistence money and cost of implements, and credited with the value of the tobacco brought in and any wages that may be due for outside work. Each estate possesses a hospital, in which bad cases are treated by a qualified practitioner, while in trifling cases the European overseer dispenses drugs, quinine being that in most demand. If, owing to sickness, or other cause, the cooly has required assistance in his field, the cost thereof is deducted in his final account.

The men live in well constructed "barracks," erected by the owner of the estate, and it is one of the duties of the Chinese "tindals," or overseers acting under the Europeans to see that they are kept in a cleanly, sanitary condition.

The European overseers are under the orders of the head manager, and an estate is divided in such a way that each overseer shall have under his direct control and be responsible for the proper cultivation of about 100 fields. He receives a fixed salary, but his interest in his division is augmented by the fact that he will receive a commission on the value of the crop it produces. His work is onerous and, during the season, he has little time to himself, but should be here, there, and everywhere in his division, seeing that the coolies come out to work at the stated times, that no field is allowed to get in a backward state, and that worms are carefully removed, and, as a large proportion of the men are probably *sinkehs*, that is, new arrivals who have never been on a tobacco estate before, he has, with the assistance of the tindals, to instruct them in their work. When the crop is brought in, he has to examine each cooly's contribution, carefully inspecting each leaf, and keeping an account of the value and quantity of each.

Physical strength, intelligence and an innate desire of amasing dollars, are three essential qualifications for a good tobacco cooly, and, so far, they have only been found united in the Chinaman, the European being out of the question as a field-labourer in the tropics.

The coolies are, as a rule, procured through Chinese cooly brokers in Penang or Singapore, but as regards North Borneo, the charges for commission, transport and the advances—many of which, owing to death, sickness and desertion, are never repaid—have become so heavy as to be almost prohibitive, and my energetic friend, Count GELOES, has set the example of procuring his coolies direct from China, instead of by the old fashioned, roundabout way of the extortionate labour-brokers of the Straits Settlements. North Borneo, it will be remembered, is situated midway between Hongkong and Singapore, and the Court of Directors of the Governing Company could do nothing better calculated to ensure the success of their public-spirited enterprise than to inaugurate regular, direct steam communication between their territory and Hongkong. In the first instance, this could only be effected by a Government subsidy or guarantee, but it is probable that, in a short time, a cargo and passenger traffic would grow up which would permit of the subsidy being gradually withdrawn.

Many of the best men on a well managed estate will re-engage themselves on the expiration of their term of agreement, receiving a fresh advance, and some of them can be trusted to go back to China and engage their clansmen for the estate.

In British North Borneo the general welfare of the indentured coolies is looked after by Government Officials, who act under the provisions of a law entitled "The Estate Coolies and Labourers Protection Proclamation, 1883."

Owing to the expense of procuring coolies and to the fact that every operation of tobacco planting must be performed punctually at the proper season of the year, and to the desirability of encouraging coolies to re-engage themselves, it is manifestly the planters' interest to treat his employés well, and to provide, so far as possible, for their health and comfort on the estate, but, notwithstanding all the care that may be taken, a considerable amount of sickness and many deaths must be allowed for on tobacco estates, which, as a rule, are opened on virgin soil; for, so long as there remains any untouched land on his estate, the planter rarely makes use of land off which a crop has been taken.

In North Borneo the jungle is generally felled towards the end of the wet season, and planting commences in April or May. The Native Dusun, Sulu and Brunai labour is available for jungle-felling and house-building, and *nibong* palms for posts and *nipa* palms for thatch, walls and *kajangs* exist in abundance.

· Writing to the Court of Directors in 1884 I said :—" The experiment in the Suanlambah conclusively proves so far that this country will do for tobacco.* * * * There seems every reason to conclude that it will do as well here as in Sumatra. When this fact becomes known, I presume there will be quite a small rush to the country, as the Dutch Government, I hear, is not popular in Sumatra, and land available for tobacco there is becoming scarcer."

My anticipations have been verified, and the rush is already taking place.

The localities at present in favour with tobacco planters are Marudu Bay and Banguey Island in the North, Labuk Bay and Darvel Bay in the neighbourhood of the Silam Station, and the Kinabatangan River on the East

The firstcomers obtained their land on very easy terms, some of them at 30 cents an acre, but the Court has now issued an order that in future no planting land is to be disposed of for a less sum than $1* per acre, free of quit-rent and on a lease for 999 years, with clauses providing that a certain proportion be brought under cultivation.

At present no export duty is levied on tobacco shipped from North Borneo, and the Company has engaged that no such duty shall be imposed before the 1st January, 1892, after which date it will be optional with them to levy an export royalty at the rate of one dollar cent, or a halfpenny, per lb., which rate, they promise, shall not be exceeded during the succeeding twenty years.

The tobacco cultivated in Sumatra and British North Borneo is used chiefly for wrappers for cigars, for which purpose a very fine, thin, elastic leaf is required and one that has a good colour and will burn well and evenly, with a fine white ash. This quality of leaf commands a much higher price than ordinary kinds, and, as stated, Count GELOES' trial crop, from the Ranan Estate in Marudu Bay, averaged 1.83 guilders, or about $1 (3/2) per lb. It is said that 2 lbs. or 2½ lbs. weight of Bornean tobacco will cover 1,000 cigars.

Tobacco is not a new culture in Borneo, as some of the hill natives on the West Coast of North Borneo have grown it in a rough and ready way for years past, supplying the population of Brunai and surrounding districts with a sun-dried article, which used to be preferred to that produced in Java. The Malay name for tobacco is *tambako*, a corruption of the

---

* Raised in 1890 to $6 an acre.

Spanish and Portuguese term, but the Brunai people also know it as *sigup*.

It was probably introduced into Malay countries by the Portuguese, who conquered Malacca in 1511, and by the Spanish, who settled in the Philippines in 1565. Its use has become universal with men, women and children, of all tribes and of all ranks. The native mode of using tobacco has been referred to in my description of Brunai.

Fibre-yielding plants are also now attracting attention in North Borneo, especially the Manila hemp (*Musa textilis*) a species of banana, and pine-apples, both of which grow freely. The British Borneo Trading and Planting Company have acquired the patent for Borneo of DEATH'S fibre-cleaning machines, and are experimenting with these products on a considerable scale and, apparently, with good prospects of success.* For a long time past, beautiful cloths have been manufactured of pine-apple fibre in the Philippines, and as it is said that orders have been received from France for Borneo pine-apple fibre, we shall perhaps soon see it used in England under the name of French *silk*.

In the Government Experimental Garden at Silam, in Darvel Bay, cocoa, cinnamon and Liberian coffee have been found to do remarkably well. Sappan-wood and *kapok* or cotton flock also grow freely.

CHAPTER X.

Many people have a very erroneous idea of the objects and intentions of the British North Borneo Company. Some, with a dim recollection of untold wealth having been extracted from the natives of India in the early days of the Honourable East India Company, conceive that the Company can have no other object than that of fleecing our natives in order to pay dividends; but the old saying, that it is a difficult matter to steal a Highlander's pantaloons, is applicable to North Borneo, for only a magician could extract anything much worth having in the shape of loot from the easy going natives

---

* The anticipated success has not been achieved as yet.

of the country, who, in a far more practical sense than the Christians of Europe, are ready to say "sufficient for the day is the evil thereof," and who do not look forward and provide for the future, or heap up riches to leave to their posterity.

Some years ago, a correspondent of an English paper displayed his ignorance on the matter by maintaining that the Company coerced the natives and forced them to buy Manchester goods at extortionate prices. An Oxford Don, when I first received my appointment as Governor, imagined that I was going out as a sort of slave-driver, to compel the poor natives to work, without wages, on the Company's plantations. But, as a matter of fact, though entitled to do so by the Royal Charter, the Company has elected to engage neither in trade nor in planting, deeming that their desire to attract capital and population to their territory will be best advanced by their leaving the field entirely open to others, for otherwise there would always have been a suspicion that rival traders and planters were handicapped in the race with a Company which had the making and the administration of laws and the imposition of taxation in its hands.

It will be asked, then, if the Company do not make a profit out of trading, or planting, or mining, what could have induced them to undertake the Government of a tropical country, some 10,000 miles or more distant from London, for Englishmen, as a rule, do not invest hundreds of thousands of pounds with the philanthropic desire only of benefitting an Eastern race?

The answer to this question is not very plainly put in the Company's prospectus, which states that its object "is the carrying on of the work begun by the Provisional Association" (said in the previous paragraphs of the prospectus to have been the successful accomplishment of the *completion* of the pioneer work) "and the further improvement and full utilization of the vast natural resources of the country, by the introduction of new capital and labour, which they intend shall be stimulated, aided and protected by a just, humane and enlightened Government. The benefits likely to flow from the accomplishment of this object, in the opening up of new fields of tropical agriculture, new channels of enterprise, and new markets for the world's manufactures, are great and incontestable." I quite agree with the framer of the prospectus that these benefits are great and incontestable, but then they would be benefits conferred on the world at large at the expense of the shareholders of the Company, and I presume that the source from which the shareholders are to be recouped is the surplus revenues which a wisely administered Government would ensure, by judiciously fostering colonisation, principally by Chinese, by the sale of the vast acreages of "waste" or Government lands, by leasing the right to work the valuable timber forests and such minerals as may be found to exist in workable quantities, by customs duties and the "farming out" of the exclusive right to sell opium, spirits, tobacco, etc., and by other methods of raising revenue in vogue in the Eastern Colonies of the Crown. In fact, the sum invested by the shareholders is to be considered in the light of a loan to the Colony—its public debt—to be repaid with interest as the resources of the country are developed. Without encroaching on land worked, or owned by the natives, the Company has a large area of unoccupied land which it can dispose of for the highest price obtainable. That this must be the case is evident from a comparison with the Island of Ceylon, where Government land sales are still held. The area of North Borneo, it has been seen, is larger than that of Ceylon, but its population is only about 160,000, while that of Ceylon is returned as 2,825,000; furthermore, notwithstanding this comparatively large population, it is said that the land under cultivation in Ceylon forms only about one-fifth of its total area. From what I have said of the prospects of tobacco-planting in British North Borneo, it will be understood that land is being rapidly taken up, and the Company will soon be in a position to increase its selling price. Town and station lands are sold under different conditions to that for planting purposes, and are restricted as a rule to lots of the size of 66 feet by 33 feet. The lease is for 999 years, but there is an annual quit-rent at the rate of $6 per lot, which is redeemable at fifteen years' purchase. At Sandakan, lots of this size have at auction realized a premium of $350. In all cases, coal, minerals, precious stones, edible nests and guano are reserved to the Government, and, in order to protect the native proprietors, it is provided that any foreigner desirous of purchasing land from a native must do so through the Government.

Titles and mutations of titles to land are carefully registered and recorded in the Land Office, under the provisions of the Hongkong Registration of Documents Ordinance, which has been adopted in the State.

The local Government is administered by a Governor, selected by the Court of Directors subject to the approval of the Secretary of State for the Colonies. He is empowered to enact laws, which require confirmation by the Court, and is assisted in his executive functions by a Government Secretary, Residents, Assistant Residents, a Treasurer-General, a Commissioner of Lands, a Superintendent of Public Works, Commandant, Postmaster-General and other Heads of Departments usually to be found in Crown Colonies, and the British Colonial Regulations are adhered to as closely as circumstances admit. The title of Resident is borrowed from the Dutch Colonies, and the duties of the post are analogous to those of the Resident Councillors of Penang or Malacca, under the Governor of Singapore, or of the Government Agents in Ceylon. The Governor can also call to assist him in his deliberations a Council of Advice, composed of some of the Heads of Departments and of natives of position nominated to seats therein.

The laws are in the form of "Proclamations" issued by the Governor under the seal of the Territory. Most of the laws are adaptations, in whole or in part, of Ordinances enacted in Eastern Colonies, such as the Straits Settlements, Hongkong, Labuan and Fiji.

The Indian Penal Code, the Indian Codes of Civil and Criminal Procedure and the Indian Evidence and Contract Acts have been adopted in their entirety, "so far as the same shall be applicable to the circumstances of this Territory."

The Proclamation making these and other Acts the law in North Borneo was the first formal one issued, and bears date the 23rd December, 1881.

The law relating to the protection of estate coolies and labourers has been already referred to.

The question of domestic slavery was one of the first with which the Company had to grapple, the Royal Charter having ordained that " the Company shall to the best of its power discourage and, as far as may be practicable, abolish by hegrees, any system of domestic servitude existing among the tribes of the Coast or interior of Borneo; and no foreigners whether European, Chinese or other, shall be allowed to own slaves of any kind in the Company's territories." Slavery and kidnapping were rampant in North Borneo under native regime and were one of the chief obstacles to the unanimous acceptance of the Company's rule by the Chiefs. At first the Residents and other officers confined their efforts to prohibiting the importation of slaves for sale, and in assisting slaves who were ill-treated to purchase their liberty. In 1883, a Proclamation was issued which will have the effect of gradually abolishing the system, as required by the Charter. Its chief provisions are as follows :—No foreigners are allowed to hold slaves, and no slaves can be imported for sale, nor can the natives buy slaves in a foreign country and introduce them into Borneo *as slaves*, even should there be no intention of selling them as such. Slaves taking refuge in the country from abroad will not be surrendered, but slaves belonging to natives of the country will be given up to their owners unless they can prove ill-treatment, or that they have been brought into the territory subsequently to the 1st November, 1883, and it is optional for any slave to purchase his or her freedom by payment of a sum, the amount of which is to be fixed, from time to time, by the Government.

A woman also becomes free if she can prove that she has cohabited with her master, or with any person other than her husband, with the connivance of her master or mistress ; and finally "all children born of slave parents after the first day of November, 1883, and who would by ancient custom be deemed to be slaves, are hereby proclaimed to be free, and any person treating or attempting to treat any such children as slaves shall be guilty of an offence under this Proclamation." The punishment for offences against the provisions of this Proclamation extends to imprisonment for ten years and to a fine up to five thousand dollars.

The late Mr. WITTI, one of the first officers of the Association, at my request, drew up, in 1881, an interesting report on the system of Slavery in force in the Tampassuk District, on the West Coast, of which the following is a brief summary. Slaves in this district are divided into two classes—those who are slaves in a strict and rigorous sense, and those whose servitude is of a light description. The latter are known as *anak mas*, and are the children of a slave mother by a free man other than her master. If a female, she is the slave or *anak mas* of her mother's master, but cannot be sold by him; if a boy, he is practically free, cannot be sold and, if he does not care to stay with his master, can move about and earn his own living, not sharing his earnings with his master, as is the case in some other districts. In case of actual need, however, his master can call upon him for his services.

If an *anak mas* girl marries a freeman, she at once becomes a free woman, but a *brihan*, or marriage gift, of from two to two and a half pikuls of brass gun—valued at $20 to $25 a pikul—is payable by the bridegroom to the master.

If she marry a slave, she remains an *anak mas*, but such cases are very rare and only take place when the husband is in a condition to pay a suitable *brihan* to the owner.

If an ordinary slave woman becomes *enceinte* by her owner, she and her offspring are henceforth free and, she may remain as one of her late master's wives. But the jealousy of the inmates of the harem often causes abortion to be procured.

The slaves, as a rule, have quite an easy time of it, living with and, as their masters, sharing the food of the family and being supplied with tobacco, betel-nut and other native luxuries. There is no difference between them and free men in the matter of dress, and in the arms which all carry, and the mere fact that they are allowed to wear arms is pretty conclusive evidence of their not being bullied or oppressed.

They assist in domestic duties and in the operations of harvest and trading and so forth, but there is no such institution as a slave-gang, working under task masters, a picture which is generally present to the Englishman's mind when he hears of the existence of slavery. The slave gang was an institution of the white slave-owner. Slave couples, provided they support themselves, are allowed to set up house and cultivate a patch of land.

For such minor offences as laziness and attempting to escape, the master can punish his slaves with strokes of the rattan, but if an owner receives grave provocation and kills his slave, the matter will probably not be taken notice of by the elders of the village.

An incorrigble slave is sometimes punished by being sold out of the district.

If a slave is badly treated and insufficiently provided with food, his offence in endeavouring to escape is generally condoned by public opinion. If a slave is, without sufficient cause, maltreated by a freeman, his master can demand compensation from the agressor. Slaves of one master can, with their owner's consent, marry, and no *brihan* is demanded, but if they belong to different masters, the woman's master is entitled to a *brihan* of one pikul, equal to $20 or $25. They continue to be the slaves of their respective masters, but are allowed to live together, and in case of a subsequent separation they return to the houses of their masters. Should a freeman, other than her master, wish to marry a slave, he practically buys her from her owner with a *brihan* of $60 or $75.

Sometimes a favourite slave is raised to a position intermediate between that of an ordinary slave and an *anak mas*, and is regarded as a brother, or sister, father, mother, or child; but if he or she attempt to escape, a reversion to the condition of an ordinary slave is the result. Occasionally, slaves are given their freedom in fulfilment of a vow to that effect made by the master in circumstances of extreme danger, experienced in company with the slave.

A slave once declared free can never be claimed again by his former master.

Debts contracted by a slave, either in his own name, or in that of his master, are not recoverable.

By their own extra work, after performing their service to their owners, slaves can acquire private property and even themselves purchase and own slaves.

Infidel slaves, of both sexes, are compulsorily converted to Muhammadanism and circumcized and, even though they should recover their freedom, they seldom relapse.

There are, or rather were, a large number of debt slaves in North Borneo. For a debt of three pikuls—$60 to $75—a man might be enslaved if his friends could not raise the requisite sum, and he would continue to be a slave until the debt was paid, but, as a most usurious interest was charged, it was almost always a hopeless task to attempt it.

Sometimes an inveterate gambler would sell himself to pay off his debts of honour, keeping the balance if any.

The natives, regardless of the precepts of the Koran, would purchase any slaves that were offered for sale, whether infidel or Muhammadan. The importers were usually the Illanun and Sulu kidnappers, who would bring in slaves of all tribes—Bajaus, Illanuns, Sulus, Brunais, Manilamen, natives of Palawan and natives of the interior of Magindanau—all was fish that came into their net. The selling price was as follows :— A boy, about 2 pikuls, a man 3 pikuls. A girl, 3 to 4 pikuls, a young woman, 3 to 5 pikuls. A person past middle age about 1½ pikuls. A young couple, 7 to 8 pikuls, an old couple, about 5 pikuls. The pikul was then equivalent to $20 or $25. Mr. WITTI further stated that in Tampassuk the proportion of free men to slaves was only one in three, and in Marudu Bay only one in five. In Tampassuk there were more female than male slaves.

Mr. A. H. EVERETT reported that, in his district of Pappar-Kimanis, there was no slave *trade*, and that the condition of the domestic slaves was not one of hardship.

Mr. W. B. PRYER, speaking for the East Coast, informed me that there were only a few slaves in the interior, mostly Sulus who had been kidnapped and sold up the rivers. Among the Sulus of the coast, the relation was rather that of follower and lord than of slave and master. When he first settled at Sandakan, he could not get men to work for him for wages, they deemed it *degrading* to do so, but they said they would work for him if he would *buy* them! Sulu, under Spanish influence, and Bulungan, in Dutch Borneo, were the chief slave markets, but the Spanish and Dutch are gradually suppressing this traffic.

There was a colony of Illanuns and Balinini settled at Tunku and Teribas on the East Coast, who did a considerable business in kidnapping, but in 1879 Commander E. EDWARDS, in H. M. S. *Kestrel*, attacked and burnt their village, capturing and burning several piratical boats and prahus.

Slavery, though not yet extinct in Borneo, has received a severe check in British North Borneo and in Sarawak, and is rapidly dying out in both countries; in fact it is a losing business to be a slave-owner now.

Apart from the institution of slavery, which is sanctioned by the Muhammadan religion, the religious customs and laws of the various tribes "especially with respect to the holding, " possession, transfer and disposition of lands and goods, and " testate or intestate succession thereto, and marriage, divorce " and legitimacy, and the rights of property and personal " rights" are carefully regarded by the Company's Government, as in duty bound, according to the terms of Articles 8 and 9 of the Royal Charter. The services of native headmen are utilised as much as possible, and Courts composed of Native Magistrates have been established, but at the same time efforts are made to carry the people with the Government in ameliorating and advancing their social position, and thus involves an amendment of some of the old customs and laws.

Moreover, customs which are altogether repugnant to modern ideas are checked or prohibited by the new Government; as, for example, the time-honoured custom of a tribe periodically balancing the account of the number of heads taken or lost by it from or to another tribe, an audit which, it is strange to say, almost invariably results in the discovery on the part of the stronger tribe that they are on the wrong side of the account and have a balance to get from the others. These hitherto interminable feuds, though not altogether put a stop to in the interior, have been in many districts effectually brought to an end, Government officers having been asked by the natives themselves to undertake the examination of the accounts and the tribe who was found to be on the debtor side paying, not human heads, but compensation in goods at a fixed rate per head due. Another custom which the Company found it impossible to recognize was that of *summungap*, which was, in reality, nothing but a form of human sacrifice, the victim being a slave bought for the purpose, and the object being to send a message to a deceased relative. With this object in view, the slave used to be bound and wrapped in cloth, when the relatives would dance round him and each thrust a spear a short way into his body, repeating, as he did so, the message which he wished conveyed. This operation was performed till the slave succumbed.

The Muhammadan practice of cutting off the hair of a woman convicted of adultery, or of men flogging her with a rattan, and that of cutting off the head of a thief, have also not received the recognition of the Company's Government.

It has been shewn that the native population of North Borneo is very small, only about five to the square mile, and as the country is fertile and well-watered and possesses, for the tropics, a healthy climate, there must be some exceptional cause for the scantiness of the population. This is to be found chiefly in the absence, already referred to, of any strong central Government in former days, and to the consequent presence of all forms of lawlessness, piracy, slave-trading, kidnapping and head-hunting.

In more recent years, too, cholera and small-pox have made frightful ravages amongst the natives, almost annihilating some of the tribes, for the people knew of no remedies and, on the approach of the scourge, deserted their homes and their sick and fled to the jungle, where exposure and privation rendered them more than ever liable to the disease. Since the Company's advent, efforts are being successfully made to introduce vaccination, in which most of the people now have confidence.

This fact of a scanty native population has, in some ways, rendered the introduction of the Company's Government a less arduous undertaking than it might otherwise have proved, and has been a fortunate circumstance for the shareholders, who have the more unowned and virgin land to dispose of.

In British North Borneo, luckily for the Company, there is not, as there is in Sarawak, any one large, powerful tribe, whose presence might have been a source of trouble, or even of danger to the young Government, but the aborigines are split up into a number of petty tribes, speaking very distinct dialects and, generally, at enmity amongst themselves, so that a general coalition of the bad elements amongst them is impossible.

The institution and amusement of head-hunting appears never to have been taken up and followed with so much energy and zeal in North Borneo as among the Dyaks of Sarawak. I do not think that it was as a rule deemed absolutely essential with any of our tribes that a young man should have taken at least a head or two before he could venture to aspire to the hand of the maiden who had led captive his heart. The heads of slain enemies were originally taken by the conquerors as a substantial proof and trophy of their successful prowess, which could not be gainsaid, and it came, in time, to be considered the proper thing to be able to boast of the possession of a large number of these ghastly tokens; and so an ambitious youth, in his desire for applause, would not be particularly careful from whom, or in what manner he obtained a head, and the victim might be, not only a person with whom he had no quarrel, but even a member of a friendly tribe, and the mode of acquisition might be, not by a fair stand-up fight, a test of skill and courage, but by treachery and ambush. Nor did it make very much difference whether the head obtained was that of a man, a woman or a child, and in their petty wars it was even conceived to be an honourable distinction to bring in the heads of women and children, the reasoning being that the men of the attacked tribe must have fought their best to defend their wives and children.

The following incident, which occurred some years ago at the Colony of Labuan, serves to shew how immaterial it was whether a friend, or foe, or utter stranger was the victim. A Murut chief of the Trusan, a river on the mainland over against Labuan, was desirous of obtaining some fresh heads on the occasion of a marriage feast, and put to sea to a district inhabited by a hostile tribe. Meeting with adverse winds, his canoes were blown over to the British Colony; the Muruts landed, held apparently friendly intercourse with some of the Kadaian (Muhammadan) population and, after a visit of two or three days, made preparations to sail; but meeting a Kadaian returning to his home alone, they shot him and went off with his head—though the man was an entire stranger to them, and they had no quarrel with any of his tribe.

With the assistance of the Brunai authorities, the chief and several of his accomplices were subsequently secured and sent for trial to Labuan. The chief died in prison, while awaiting trial, but one or two of his associates paid the penalty of their wanton crime.

A short time afterwards, Mr. COOK and I visited the Lawas River for sport, and took up our abode in a Murut long house, where, I remember, a large basket of skulls was placed as an ornament at the head of my sleeping place. One night, when all our men, with the exception of my Chinese servant, were away in the jungle, trying to trap the then newly discovered "Bulwer pheasant," some Muruts from the Trusan came over and informed our hosts of the fate of their chief. On the receipt of this intelligence, all the men of our house left it and repaired to one adjoining, where a great "drink" was held, while the women indulged in a loud, low, monotonous, heart-breaking wail, which they kept up for several hours. Mr. COOK and myself agreed that things looked almost as bad for us as they well could, and when, towards morning, the men returned to our house, my Chinese boy clung to me in terror and—nothing happened! But certainly I do not think I have ever passed such an uncomfortable period of suspense.

Writing to the Court of Directors of the East India Company a hundred and thirteen years ago, Mr. YESSE, who concluded the pepper monopoly agreement with the Brunai Government, referring to the Murut predilection for head-hunting says:—
"With respect to the Idaan, or Muruts, as they are called here, I cannot give any account of their disposition; but from what I have heard from the Borneyans, they are a set of abandoned idolaters; one of their tenets, so strangely inhuman, I cannot pass unnoticed, which is, that their future in-

terest depends upon the number of their fellow creatures they have killed in any engagement, or common disputes, and count their degrees of happiness to depend on the number of human skulls in their possession; from which, and the wild, disorderly life they lead, unrestrained by any bond of civil society, we ought not to be surprised if they are of a cruel and vindictive disposition." I think this is rather a case of giving a dog a bad name.

I heard read once at a meeting of the Royal Geographical Society, an eloquent paper on the Natives of the Andaman Islands, in which the lecturer, after shewing that the Andamanese were suspicious, treacherous, blood-thirsty, ungrateful and untruthful, concluded by giving it as his opinion that they were very good fellows and in many ways superior to white man.

I do not go quite so far as he does, but I must say that many of the aborigines are very pleasant good-natured creatures, and have a lot of good qualities in them, which, with care and discriminating legislation on the part of their new rulers, might be gradually developed, while the evil qualities which they possess in common with all races of men, might be *pari passu* not extinguished, but reduced to a minimum. But this result can only be secured by officers who are naturally of a sympathetic disposition and ready to take the trouble of studying the natives and entering into their thoughts and aspirations.

In many instances, the Company has been fortunate in its choice of officials, whose work has brought them into intimate connection with the aborigines.

A besetting sin of young officers is to expect too much— they are conscious that their only aim is to advance the best interests of the natives, and they are surprised and hurt at, what they consider, the want of gratitude and backwardness in seconding their efforts evinced by them. They forget that the people are as yet in the schoolboy stage, and should try and remember how, in their own schoolboy days, they offered opposition to the efforts of their masters for *their* improvement, and how little gratitude they felt, at the time, for all that was done for them. Patience and sympathy are the two qualifications especially requisite in officers selected for the management of native affairs.

In addition to the indigenous population, there are, settled along the coast and at the mouths of the principal rivers, large numbers of the more highly civilized tribes of Malays, of whose presence in Borneo an explanation has been attempted on a previous page. They are known as Brunais—called by the Natives, for some unexplained reason, *orang abai*—Sulus, Bajows, Illanuns and Balininis; there are also a few Bugis, or natives of Celebes.

These are the people who, before the Company's arrival, lorded it over the more ignorant interior tribes, and prevented their having direct dealings with traders and foreigners, and to whom, consequently, the advent of a still more civilized race than themselves was very distasteful.

The habits of the Brunai people have already been sufficiently described.

The Sulus are, next to the Brunais, the most civilized race and, without any exception, the most warlike and powerful. For nearly three centuries, they have been more or less in a state of war with the Spaniards of the Philippine Islands, and even now, though the Spaniards have established a fortified port in their principal island, their subjugation is by no means complete.

The Spanish officials dare not go beyond the walls of their settlement, unless armed and in force, and it is no rare thing for fanatical Sulus, singly or in small parties, to make their way into the Spanish town, under the guise of unarmed and friendly peasants, and then suddenly draw their concealed krises and rush with fury on officers, soldiers and civilians, generally managing to kill several before they are themselves cut down.

They are a much bolder and more independent race than the Brunais, who have always stood in fear of them, and it was in consideration of its undertaking to defend them against their attacks that the Brunai Government conceded the exclusive trade in pepper to the East India Company. Their religion—Muhammadanism—sits even more lightly on the Sulus than on the Brunais, and their women, who are fairer and better looking than their Brunai sisters, are never secluded or veiled, but often take part in public deliberations and, in matters of business, are even sharper than the men.

The Sulus are a bloodthirsty and hard-hearted race, and, when an opportunity occurs, are not always averse to kidnapping even their own countrymen and selling them into slavery. They entertain a high notion of their own importance, and are ever ready to resent with their krises the slightest affront which they may conceive has been put upon them.

In Borneo, they are found principally on the North-East Coast, and a good many have settled in British North Borneo under the Company's Government. They occasionally take contracts for felling jungle and other work of similar character, but are less disposed than the Brunai men to perform work for Europeans on regular wages. Among their good qualities, it may be mentioned that they are faithful and trustworthy followers of any European to whom they may become attached. Their language is distinct from ordinary Malay, and is akin to that of the Bisaias, one of the principal tribes of the Philippines, and is written in the Arabic character; but many Malay terms have been adopted into the language, and most of the trading and seafaring Sulus know enough Malay to conclude a bargain.

The most numerous Muhammadan race in British North Borneo is that of the Bajows, who are found on both coasts, but, on the West Coast, not South of the Pappar River. These are the *orang-laut* (men of the sea) or sea-gipsies of the old writers, and are the worst class that we have to deal with, being of a treacherous and thievish disposition, and confirmed gamblers and cattle-lifters.

They also form a large proportion of the population of the Sulu Islands, where they are, or used to be, noted kidnappers and pirates, though also distinguished for their skill in pearl fisheries. Their religion is that of Mahomet and their language Malay mixed, it is said, with Chinese and Japanese elements; their women are not secluded, and it is a rare thing for a Borneo Bajow to take the trouble of making the pilgrimage to Mecca. They are found along the coasts of nearly all the Malay Islands and, apparently, in former days lived entirely in their boats. In British North Borneo, a large majority have taken to building houses and residing on the shore, but when Mr. PRYER first settled at Sandakan, there was a considerable community of them in the Bay, who had no houses at all, but were born, bred, married and died in their small canoes.

On the West Coast, the Bajows, who have for a long time been settled ashore, appear to be of smaller build and darker colour than the other Malays, with small sparkling black eyes, but on the East Coast, where their condition is more primitive, Mr. PRYER thinks they are much larger in stature and stronger and more swarthy than ordinary Malays.

On the East Coast, there are no buffaloes or horned cattle, so that the Bajows there have, or I should say *had*, to be content with kidnapping only, and as an example of their daring I may relate that in, I think, the year 1875, the Austrian Frigate *Friederich*, Captain Baron OESTERREICHER, was surveying to the South of Darvel Bay, and, running short of coal, sent an armed party ashore to cut firewood. The Bajows watched their opportunity and, when the frigate was out of sight, seized the cutter, notwithstanding the fire of the party on the shore, who expended all their ammunition in vain, and carried off the two boat-keepers, whose heads were subsequently shewn round in triumph in the neighbouring islands. Baron OESTERREICHER was unable to discover the retreat of these Bajows, and they remain unpunished to this day, and are at present numbered among the subjects of the British North Borneo Company. I have been since told that I have more than once unwittingly shaken hands and had friendly intercourse with some of them. In fairness to them I should add that it is more than probable that they mistook the *Friederich* for a vessel belonging to Spain, with whom their sovereign, the Sultan of Sulu, was at that time at war. After this incident, and by order of his Government, Baron OESTERREICHER visited Sandakan Bay and, I believe, reported that he could discover no population there other than monkeys. Altogether, he could not have carried away with him a very favourable impression of Northern Borneo. On the West Coast, gambling and cattle-lifting are the main pursuits of the gentlemanly Bajow, pursuits which soon brought him into close and very uncomfortable relations with the new Government, for which he entertains anything but feelings of affection. One of the principal independent rivers on the West Coast — *i. e.*, rivers which have not yet been ceded to the Company — is the Mengkabong, the majority of the inhabitants of which are Bajows, so that it has become a sort of river of refuge for the bad characters on the coast, as well as an entrepôt for the smuggling of gunpowder for sale to the head-hunting tribes of the interior. The existence of these independent and intermediate rivers on their West Coast is a serious difficulty for the Company in its efforts to establish good government and put down lawlessness, and every one having at heart the true interests of the natives of Borneo must hope that the Company will soon be successful in the negotiations which they have opened for the acquisition of these rivers. The Kawang was an important river, inhabited by a small number of Bajows, acquired by the Company in 1884, and the conduct of these people on one occasion affords a good idea of their treachery and their hostility towards good government. An interior tribe had made itself famous for its head-hunting proclivities, and the Kawang was selected as the best route by which to reach their district and inflict punishment upon them. The selection of this route was not a politic one, seeing that the inhabitants *were* Bajows, and that they had but recently come under the Company's rule. The expedition was detained a day or two at the Bajow village, as the full number of Dusun baggage-carriers had not arrived, and the Bajows were called upon to make up the deficiency, but did not do so. Matters were further complicated by the Dusuns recognising some noted cattle-lifters in the village, and demanding a buffalo which had been stolen from them. It being impossible to obtain the required luggage carriers, it was proposed to postpone the expedition, the stores were deposited in some of the houses of the village and the Constabulary were "dismissed" and, piling their arms, laid down under the shelter of some trees. Without any warning one of two Bajows, with whom Dr. FRASER was having an apparently friendly chat, discharged his musket point blank at the Doctor, killing him on the spot, and seven others rushed among the unarmed

Constables and speared the Sikh Jemmadhar and the Sergeant-Major and a private and then made off for the jungle. Captain DE FONTAINE gallantly, but rashly started off in pursuit, before any one could support him. He tripped and fell and was so severely wounded by the Bajows, after killing three of them with his revolver, that he died a few days afterwards at Sandakan. By this time the Sikhs had got their rifles and firing on the retreating party killed three and wounded two. Assistant Resident LITTLE, who had received a spear in his arm, shot his opponent dead with his revolver. None of the other villagers took any active part, and consequently were only punished by the imposition of a fine. They subsequently all cleared out of the Company's territory. It was a sad day for the little Colony at Sandakan when Mr. WHITEHEAD, a naturalist who happened to be travelling in the neighbourhood at the time, brought us the news of the melancholy affray, and the wounded Captain DE FONTAINE and several Sikhs, to whose comfort and relief he had, at much personal inconvenience, attended on the tedious voyage in a small steam-launch from the Kawang to the Capital. On the East Coast, also, their slave-dealing and kidnapping propensities brought the Bajows into unfriendly relations with the Government, and their lawlessness culminated in their kidnapping several Eraan birds' nest collectors, whom they refused to surrender, and making preparations for resisting any measures which might be taken to coerce them. As these same people had, a short time previously, captured at sea some five Dutch subjects, it was deemed that their offences brought them within the cognizance of the Naval authorities, and Captain A. K. HOPE, R.N., at my request, visited the district, in 1886, in H. M. S. *Zephyr* and, finding that the people of two of the Bajow villages refused to hold communication with us, but prepared their boats for action, he opened fire on them under the protection of which a party of the North Borneo Constabulary landed and destroyed the villages, which were quickly deserted, and many of the boats which had been used on piratical excursions. Happily, there was no loss of life on either side, and a very wholesome and useful lesson was given to the pirates without the shedding of blood, thanks to the good arrangements and tact of Captain HOPE In order that the good results of this lesson should not be wasted, I revisited the scene of the little engagement in the *Zepyhyr* a few weeks subsequently, and not long afterwards the British flag was again shewn in the district, by Captain A. H. ALINGTON in H. M. S. *Satellite*, who interviewed the offending chiefs and gave them sound advice as to their conduct in future.

Akin to the Bajows are the Illanuns and Balinini, Muhammadan peoples, famous in former days as the most enterprising pirates of the Malayan seas. The Balinini, Balignini or Balanguini—as their name is variously written—originally came from a small island to the north of Sulu, and the Illanuns from the south coast of the island of Mindanao—one of the Philippines, but by the action of the Spanish and British cruisers their power has been broken and they are found scattered in small numbers throughout the Sulu Islands and on the seaboard of Northern Borneo, on the West Coast of which they founded little independent settlements, arrogating to their petty chiefs such high sounding titles as Sultan, Maharajah and so forth.

The Illanuns are a proud race and distinguished by wearing a much larger sword than the other tribes, with a straight blade about 28 inches in length. This sword is called a *kampilan*, and is used in conjunction with a long, narrow, wooden shield, known by the name of *klassap*, and in the use of these weapons the Illanuns are very expert and often boast that, were it not for their gunpowder, no Europeans could stand up to them, face to face. I believe, that it is these people who in former days manufactured the chain armour of which I have seen several specimens, but the use of which has now gone out of fashion. Those I have are made of small brass rings linked together, and with plates of brass or buffalo horn in front. The headpiece is of similar construction.

There are no Negritos in Borneo, although they exist in the Malay Peninsula and the Philippines, and our explorers have failed to obtain any specimens of the "tailed" people in whose existence many of the Brunai people believe. The late Sultan of Brunai gravely assured me that there was such a tribe, and that the individuals composing it were in the habit of carrying about chairs with them, in the seat of each of which there was a little hole, in which the lady or gentleman carefully inserted her or his tail before settling down to a comfortable chat. This belief in the existence of a tailed race appears to be widespread, and in his " Pioneering in New Guinea" Mr. CHALMERS gives an amusing account of a detailed description of such a tribe by a man who vowed *he had lived with them*, and related how they were provided with long sticks, with which to make holes in the ground before squatting down, for the reception of their short stumpy tails! I think it is Mr. H. F. ROMILLY who, in his interesting little work on the Western Pacific and New Guinea, accounts for the prevalence of " yarns" of this class by explaining that the natives regard Europeans as being vastly superior to them in general knowledge and, when they find them asking such questions as, for instance, whether there are tailed-people in the interior, jump to the conclusion that the white men must have good grounds for believing that they do exist, and then they gradually come to believe in their existence themselves. There is, however, I think, some excuse for the Brunai people's belief, for I have seen one tribe of Muruts who, in addition to the usual small loin cloth, wear on their backs only a skin of a long-tailed monkey, the tail of which hangs down behind in such a manner as, when the men are a little distance off, to give one at first glance the impression that it is part and parcel of the biped.

In Labuan it used to be a very common occurrence for the graves of the Europeans, of which unfortunately, owing to its bad climate when first settled, there are a goodly number, to be found desecrated and the bones scattered about. The perpetrators of these outrages have never been discovered, notwithstanding the most stringent enquiries. It was once thought that they were broken open by head-hunting tribes from the mainland, but this theory was disproved by the fact that the skulls were never carried away. As we know of no Borneo tribe which is in the habit of breaking open graves, the only conclusion that can be come to is that the graves were rifled under the supposition that the Europeans buried treasure with their dead, though it is strange that their experiences of failure never seemed to teach them that such was not the case.

The Muhammadan natives are buried in the customary Muhammadan manner in regular graveyards kept for the purpose.

The aborigines generally bury their dead near their houses, erecting over the graves little sheds adorned, in the case of chiefs, with bright coloured clothes, umbrellas, etc. I once went to see the lying in state of a deceased Datoh, who had been dead nine days. On entering the house I looked about for the corpse in vain, till my attention was drawn to an old earthen jar, tilted slightly forward, on the top of the old Chief's goods—his sword, spear, gun and clothing.

In this jar were the Datoh's remains, the poor old fellow having been doubled up, head and heels together, and forced through the mouth of the vessel, which was about two feet in diameter. The jar itself was about four feet high. Over the corpse was thickly sprinkled the native camphor, and the jar was closed with a piece of buffalo hide, well sealed over with gum dammar. They told us the Datoh was dressed in his best clothes and had his pipe with him, but nothing else. He was to be buried that day in a small grave excavated near the house, just large enough to contain the jar, and a buffalo was being killed and intoxicating drink prepared for the numerous friends and followers who were flocking in for the wake. Over his grave cannon would be fired to arouse the spirits who were to lead him to Kinabalu, the people shouting out "Turn neither to the right nor to the left, but proceed straight to Kinabalu"—the sacred mountain where are collected the spirits of all good Dusuns under, I believe, the presidency of a great spirit known as Kinaringan.

Chapter XI.

The population of North Borneo, as has been shewn, is very scanty, and the great object of the new Government should be to attract population and capital to their territory. Java is often quoted as an island which, under Dutch rule, has attained great prosperity without any large immigration of Chinese or other foreigners. This is true, but in Java the Dutch had not only a fertile soil and good climate in their favour, but found their Colony already thickly populated by native races who had, under Hindu and Arab influences, made considerable advances in civilization, in trade and in agriculture, and who, moreover, had been acccustomed to a strong Government.

The Dutch, too, were in those days able to introduce a Government of a paternal and despotic character which the British North Borneo Company are, by the terms of the Royal Charter, precluded from imitating.

It was Sir JAMES BROOKE'S wish to keep Sarawak for the natives, but his successor has recognised the impolicy of so doing and admits that "without the Chinese we can do nothing." Experience in the Straits Settlements, the Malay Peninsula and Sarawak has shewn that the people to cause rapid financial progress in Malayan countries are the hardworking, money-loving Chinese, and these are the people whom the Company should lay themselves out to attract to Borneo, as I have more than once pointed out in the course of these remarks. It matters not what it is that attracts them to the country, whether trade, as in Singapore, agriculture, as in Johor and Sarawak, or mining as in Perak and other of the Protected Native States of the Peninsula—once get them to voluntarily immigrate, and govern them with firmness and justice, and the financial success of the Company would, in my opinion, be assured. The inducements for the Chinese to come to North Borneo are trade, agriculture and possibly mining. The bulk of those already in the country are traders, shop-keepers, artisans and the coolies employed by them, and the numbers introduced by the European tobacco planters for the cultivation of their estates, under the system already explained, is yearly increasing. Very few are as yet engaged in agriculture on their own account, and it must be confessed that the luxuriant tropical jungle presents considerable difficulties to an agriculturist from China, accustomed to a country devoid of forest, and it would be impossible for Chinese peasants to open land in Borneo for themselves without monetary assistance, in the first instance, from the Government or from capitalists. In Sarawak Chinese pepper planters were attracted by free passages in Government ships and by loans of money, amounting to a considerable total, nearly all of which have since been repaid, while the revenues of the State have been almost doubled. The British North Borneo Company early recognised the desirabilty of encouraging Chinese immigration, but set to work in too great haste and without judgment.

They were fortunate in obtaining the services for a short time, as their Commissioner of Chinese Immigration, of a man so well-known in China as the late Sir WALTER MEDHURST, but he was appointed before the Company's Government was securely established and before proper arrangements had been made for the reception of the immigrants, or sufficient knowledge obtained of the best localities in which to locate them. His influence and the offer of free passages from China, induced many to try their fortune in the Colony, but the majority of them were small shop-keepers, tailors, bootmakers, and artisans, who naturally could not find a profitable outlet for their energies in a newly opened country to which capital (except that of the Governing Company) had not yet been attracted, and a large proportion of the inhabitants of which were satisfied with a loin cloth as the sole article of their attire. Great, therefore, was their disappointment, and comparatively few remained to try their luck in the country. One class of these immigrants, however, took kindly to North Borneo—the Hakkas, an agricultural clan, many of whom have embraced the Christian religion and are, in consequence, somewhat looked down upon by their neighbours. They are a steady, hard-working body of men, and cultivate vegetable and coffee gardens in the vicinity of the Settlements and rear poultry and pigs. The women are steady, and work almost as well as the men. They may form a valuable factor in the colonization of the country and a source of cheap labour for the planters in the future.

Sir SPENCER ST. JOHN, formerly Her Britannic Majesty's Consul-General at Brunai and who knew Borneo well, in his preface to the second edition of his "Life in the Forests of the Far East," lays great stress on the suitability of North Borneo for the immigration of Chinese on a very large scale, and prophesied that "should the immigration once commence, it would doubtless assume great proportions and continue until every acre of useless jungle is cleared away, to give place to rice, pepper, gambier, sugar-cane, cotton, coffee, indigo and those other products which flourish on its fertile soil." No doubt a considerable impetus would be given to the immigration of Chinese and the introduction of Chinese as well as of European capital, were the British Government to proclaim* formally a Protectorate over the country, meanwhile the Company should try the effect of the offer of free passages from China and from Singapore and of liberal allotments of suitable land to *bonâ fide* agriculturists.

The sources of the Company's revenues have been referred to on a previous page, and may be summarised here under the following principal heads:—The "Farms" of Opium, Tobacco, Spirits, and of Pawnbroking, the Rent of the edible birds'-nest caves, Market Dues, Duties on Imports and Exports, Court Fines and Fees, Poll Tax on aborigines, House and Store Rents, profit accruing from the introduction of the Company's copper or bronze token coinage—a considerable item—Interest and Commission resulting from the Banking business carried on by the Treasury pending the establishment of a Banking Company, Land Sales and Quit-rents on land alienated, and Postal Receipts.

The Poll Tax is a source of revenue well-known in the East and not objected to by most of our natives, with whom it takes the place of the land rent which the Government of India imposes. To our aborigines a land rent would be most distasteful at present, and they infinitely prefer the Poll Tax and to be allowed to own and farm what land they like without paying premium or rent. The more civilized tribes, especially on the West coast, recognize private property in land, the boundaries of their gardens and fields being carefully

---

* Now accomplished.

marked and defined, and the property descending from fathers to children. The rate of the Poll Tax is usually $2 for married couples and $1 for adult bachelors per annum, and I believe this is about the same rate as that collected by the British Government in Burma. At first sight it has the appearance of a tax on marriage, but in the East generally women do a great deal of the out-door as well as of the indoor work, so that a married man is in a much better position than a bachelor for acquiring wealth, as he can be engaged in collecting jungle produce, or in trading, or in making money in other ways, while his womenkind are planting out or gathering in the harvest.

The amounts *received* by the Company for the sale of their waste lands has been as follows:—

1882,	... $ 16,340		1885,	... $ 2,860
1883,	... $ 25,449		1886,	... $12,035
1884,	... $ 15,460		1887,*	... $14,505

The receipts for 1888, owing to the rush for tobacco lands already alluded to, and to the fact that the balances of the premia on lands taken up in 1887 becomes due in that year, will be considerably larger than those of any previous period.

The most productive, and the most elastic source of revenue is that derived from the Excise on the retail of opium and, with the comparatively small number of Chinese at present in the country, this amounted in 1887 to $19,980, having been only $4,537 in 1882.† The next most substantial and promising item is the Customs Duties on Import and Export, which from about $8,300 in 1882 have increased to $19,980 in 1887.‡

The local expenditure in Borneo is chiefly for salaries of the officials, the armed Constabulary and for Gaols and Public Works, the annual "rental" payable to the Sultans of Brunai and Sulu and others, the subsidizing of steamers, Medical

---

* In 1888, $246,457.
† In 1888, $22,755 were realized, and the Estimate for 1890 is $70,000 for the Opium Farm.
‡ In 1888, $22,755.

Services, Printing, Stationery, Prospecting, Experimental Gardens and Harbour and Postal Services. The designations of the principal officials employed by the Company in Borneo have been given on a previous page; the salaries allowed them, as a rule, can scarcely be called too liberal, and unfortunately the Court of Directors does not at present feel that it is justified in sanctioning any pension scheme. Those of my readers who are conversant with the working of Public Offices will recognize that this decision of the Directors deprives the service of one great incentive to hard and continuous work and of a powerful factor in the maintenance of an effective discipline, and it speaks volumes for the quality of the officials, whose services the Company has been so fortunate as to secure without this attraction, that it is served as faithfully, energetically and zealously as any Government in the world. If I may be allowed to say so here, I can never adequately express my sense of the valuable assistance and support I received from the officers, with scarcely any exception, during my six years' tenure of the appointment of Governor. An excellent spirit pervades the service and, when the occasions have arisen, there have never been wanting officers ready to risk their lives in performing their duties, without hope of rewards or distinctions, Victoria Crosses or medals.

The figures below speak for the advance which the country is making, not very rapidly, perhaps the shareholders may think, but certainly, though slowly, surely and steadily:—

Revenue in 1883, $51,654, with the addition of Land Sales, $25,449, a total of $77,103.

Revenue in 1887, $142,687, with the addition of Land Sales, $14,505, a total of $ 157,192.

Expenditure in 1883, including expenditure on Capital Account, $391,547.

Expendiure in 1887, including expenditure on Capital Account, $209,862.

For reasons already mentioned, the revenue for 1888 is expected to considerably exceed that of any previous year, while the expenditure will probably not be more and may be less than that of 1887.*

The expenses of the London office average, I believe, about £3,000 a year.

As Sir RUTHERFORD ALCOCK, their able and conscientious Chairman, explained to the shareholders at a recent meeting, "with reference to the important question of expenditure, the position of the Company was that of a man coming into possession of a large estate which had been long neglected, and which was little better than a wilderness. If any rent roll was to be derived from such a property there must be, in the first place, a large outlay in many ways before the land could be made profitable, or indeed tenantable. That was what the Company had had to do and what they had been doing; *and that had been the history of all our Colonies.*" I trust that the few observations I have offered will have shewn my readers that, though British North Borneo might be described as a wilderness so far as regards the absence of development when the Company took possession of it, such a description is by no means applicable to it when regard is had to its great and undoubted natural resources.

British North Borneo not being a Crown Colony, it has to provide itself for the maintenance of order, both ashore and afloat, without assistance from the Imperial Army or Navy, except such temporary assistance as has been on two occasions accorded by Her Majesty's vessels, under circumstances which have been detailed. There are no Imperial Troops stationed either in Labuan or in any portion of Borneo, and the Company has organized an armed Police Force to act both in a military and in a civil capacity.

The numbers of their Force do not much exceed two hundred of all ranks, and are composed principally of Sikhs from the Punjaub and a few Dyaks from Sarawak—an excellent mixture for fighting purposes, the Dyaks being sufficiently

---

* Revenue in 1888, $148,286, with addition of Land Sales, $246,457, a total of $394,743.
Expenditure in 1888, including Padas war expenses, $210,985, and expenditure on Capital Account, $25,283—total $236,268.

courageous and expert in all the arts of jungle warfare, while the pluck and cool steadiness under fire of the Sikhs is too well-known to need comment here. The services of any number of Sikhs can, it appears, be easily obtained for this sort of work, and some years ago a party of them even took service with the native Sultan of Sulu, who, however, proved a very indifferent paymaster and was soon deserted by his mercenaries, who are the most money-grabbing lot of warriors I have ever heard of. Large bodies of Sikhs are employed and drilled as Armed Constables in Hongkong, in the Straits Settlements and in the Protected Native States of the Malay Peninsula, who, after a fixed time of service, return to their country, their places being at once taken by their compatriots, and one cannot help thinking what effect this might have in case of future disturbances in our Indian Empire, should the Sikh natives make common cause with the malcontents.

Fault has been found with the Company for not following the example of Sarawak and raising an army and police from among its own people. This certainly would have been the best policy had it only been feasible; but the attempt was made and failed.

As I have pointed out, British North Borneo is fortunate in not possessing any powerful aboriginal tribe of pronounced warlike instincts, such as the Dyaks of Sarawak.

The Muhammadan Bajows might in time make good soldiers, but my description of them will have shewn that the Company could not at present place reliance in them.

While on the subject of "fault finding," I may say that the Company has also been blamed for its expenditure on public works and on subsidies for steam communication with the outer world.

But our critics may rest assured that, had not the Company proved its faith in the country by expending some of its money on public works and in providing facilities for the conveyance of intending colonists, neither European capital nor Chinese population, so indispensable to the success of their scheme, would have been attracted to their Territory as is now being done—for the country and its new Government lacked the prestige which attaches to a Colony opened by the Imperial Government. The strange experiment, in the present day, of a London Company inaugurating a Government in a tropical Colony, perhaps not unnaturally caused a certain feeling of pique and uncharitableness in the breasts of that class of people who cannot help being pleased at the non-success of their neighbours' most cherished schemes, and who are always ready with their "I told you so." The measure of success attained by British North Borneo caused it to come in for its full share of this feeling, and I am not sure that it was not increased and aggravated by the keen interest which all the officers took in the performance of their novel duties—an interest which, quite unintentionally, manifested itself, perhaps, in a too enthusiastic and somewhat exaggerated estimate of the beauties and resources of their adopted country and of the grandeur of its future destiny and of its rapid progress, and which, so to speak, brought about a reaction towards the opposite extreme in the minds of the class to whom I refer. This enthusiasm was, to say the least, pardonable under the circumstances, for all men are prone to think that objects which intensely engross their whole attention are of more importance than the world at large is pleased to admit. Every man worth his salt thinks his own geese are swans.

A notable exception to this narrow-mindedness was, however, displayed by the Government of Singapore, especially by its present Governor, Sir CECIL CLEMENTI SMITH, who let no opportunity pass of encouraging the efforts of the infant Government by practical assistance and unprejudiced counsel.

Lord BRASSEY, whose visit to Borneo in the *Sunbeam* I have mentioned, showed a kindly appreciation of the efforts of the Company's officers, and practically evinced his faith in the future of the country by joining the Court of Directors on his return to England.

In the number of the "Nineteenth Century" for August, 1887, is a sketch of the then position of the portion of Borneo which is under the British influence, from his pen.

As the country is developed and land taken up by European planters and Chinese, the Company will be called upon for further expenditure on public works, in the shape of roads, for at present, in the interior, there exist only rough native tracks, made use of by the natives when there does not happen to be a river handy for the transport of themselves and their goods. Though well watered enough, British North Borneo possesses no rivers navigable for European vessels of any size, except perhaps the Sibuku River, the possession of which is at the present moment a subject of dispute with the the Dutch. This is due to the natural configuration of the country. Borneo, towards the North, becoming comparatively narrow and of roughly triangular shape, with the apex to the North. The only other river of any size and navigable for vessels drawing about nine feet over the bar, is the Kinabatangan, which, like the Sibuku, is on the East side, the coast range of mountains, of which Kinabalu forms a part, being at no great distance from the West coast and so preventing the occurrence of any large rivers on that side. From data already to hand, it is calculated that the proceeds of Land Sales for 1887 and 1888 will equal the total revenue from all other sources, and a portion of this will doubtless be set aside for road making and other requisite public works.

The question may be asked what has the Company done for North Borneo?

A brief reply to this question would include the following points. The Company has paved the way to the ultimate extinction of the practice of slavery; it has dealt the final blow to the piracy and kidnapping which still lingered on its coasts; it has substituted one strong and just Government for numerous weak, cruel and unjust ones; it has opened Courts of Justice which know no distinction between races and creeds, between rich and poor, between master and slave; it is rapidly adjusting ancient blood feuds between the tribes and putting a stop to the old custom of head-hunting; it has broken down the barrier erected by the coast Malays to prevent the aborigines having access to the outer world and is thus enabling trade and its accompanying civilisation to reach the interior races; and it is attracting European and Chinese capital to the country and opening a market for British traders.

These are some, and not inconsiderable ones, of the achievements of the British North Borneo Company, which, in its humble way, affords another example of the fact that the "expansion of Britain" has been in the main due not to the exertions of its Government so much as to the energy and enterprise of individual citizens, and Sir ALFRED DENT, the the founder, and Sir RUTHERFORD ALCOCK, the guide and supporter of the British North Borneo Company, cannot but feel a proud satisfaction in the reflection that their energy and patient perseverance have resulted in conferring upon so considerable a portion of the island of Borneo the benefits above enumerated and in adding another Colony to the long list of the Dependencies of the British Crown.

In the matter of geographical exploration, too, the Company and its officers have not been idle, as the map brought out by the Company sufficiently shews, for previous maps of North Borneo will be found very barren and uninteresting, the interior being almost a complete blank, though possessing one natural feature which is conspicuous by its absence in the more recent and trustworthy one, and that is the large lake of Kinabalu, which the explorations of the late Mr. F. K. WITTI have proved to be non-existent. Two explanations are given of the origin of the myth of the Kinabalu Lake—one is that in the district, where it was supposed to exist, extensive floods do take place in very wet seasons, giving it the appearance of a lake, and, I believe there are many similar instances in Dutch Borneo, where a tract of country liable to be heavily flooded has been dignified with the name of *Danau*, which is Malay for *lake*, so that the mistake of the European cartographers is a pardonable one. The other explanation is that the district in question is known to the aboriginal inhabitants as *Danau*, a word which, in their language, has no particular meaning, but which, as above stated, signifies, in Malay, a lake. The first European visitors would have gained all their information from the Malay coast tribes, and the reason for their mistaken supposition of the existence of a large lake can be readily understood. The two principal pioneer explorers of British North Borneo were WITTI and FRANK HATTON, both of whom met with violent deaths. WITTI'S services as one of the first officers stationed in the country, before the British North Borneo Company was formed, have already been referred to, and I have drawn on his able report for a short account of the slave system which formerly prevailed. He had served in the Austrian Navy and was a very energetic, courageous and accomplished man. Besides minor journeys, he had traversed the country from West to East and from North to South, and it was on his last journey from Pappar, on the West Coast, inland to the headwaters of the Kinabatangan and Sambakong Rivers, that he was murdered by a tribe, whose language none of his party understood, but whose confidence he had endeavoured to win by reposing confidence in them, to the extent even of letting them carry his carbine. He and his men had slept in the village one night, and on the following day some of the tribe joined the party as guides, but led them into the ambuscade, where the gallant WITTI and many of his men were killed by *sumpitans*.* So far as we have been able to ascertain the sole reason for the attack was the fact that WITTI had come to the district from a tribe with whom these people were at war, and he was, therefore, according to native custom, deemed also to be an enemy. FRANK HATTON joined the Company's service with the object of investigating the mineral resources of the country and in the course of his work travelled over a great portion of the Territory, prosecuting his journeys from both the West and the East coasts, and undergoing the hardships incidental to travel in a roadless, tropical country with such ability, pluck and success as surprised me in one so young and slight and previously untrained and inexperienced in rough pioneering work.

He more than once found himself in critical positions with inland tribes, who had never seen or heard of a white man, but his calmness and intrepidity carried him safely through

---

* The *sumpitan*, or native blow-pipe, has been frequently described by writers on Borneo. It is a tube 6½ feet long, carefully perforated lengthwise and through which is fired a poisoned dart, which has an extreme range of about 80 to 90 yards, but is effective at about 20 to 30 yards. It takes the place in Borneo of the bow and arrow of savage tribes, and is used only by the aborigines and not by the Muhammadan natives.

such difficulties, and with several chiefs he became a sworn brother, going through the peculiar ceremonies customary on such occasions. In 1883, he was ascending the Segama River to endeavour to verify the native reports of the existence of gold in the district when, landing on the bank, he shot at and wounded an elephant, and while following it up through the jungle, his repeating rifle caught in a rattan and went off, the bullet passing through his chest, causing almost immediate death. HATTON, before leaving England, had given promise of a distinguished scientific career, and his untimely fate was deeply mourned by his brother officers and a large circle of friends. An interesting memoir of him has been published by his father, Mr. JOSEPH HATTON, and a summary of his journeys and those of WITTI, and other explorers in British North Borneo, appeared in the "Proceedings of the Royal Geographical Society and Monthly Record of Geography" for March, 1888, being the substance of a paper read before the Society by Admiral R. C. MAYNE, C.B., M.P. A memorial cross has been erected at Sandakan, by their brother officers, to the memory of WITTI, HATTON, DE FONTAINE and Sikh officers and privates who have lost their lives in the service of the Government.

To return for a moment to the matter of fault-finding, it would be ridiculous to maintain that no mistakes have been made in launching British North Borneo on its career as a British Dependency, but then I do not suppose that any single Colony of the Crown has been, or will be inaugurated without similar mistakes occurring, such, for instance, as the withholding money where money was needed and could have been profitably expended, and a too lavish expenditure in other and less important directions. Examples will occur to every reader who has studied our Colonial history. If we take the case of the Colony of the Straits Settlements, now one of our most prosperous Crown Colonies and which was founded by the East India Company, it will be seen that in 1826-7 the "mistakes" of the administration were on such a scale that there was an annual deficit of £100,000, and the presence of the Governor-General of India was called for to abolish useless offices and effect retrenchments throughout the service.

The British North Borneo Company possesses a valuable property, and one which is daily increasing in value, and if they continue to manage it with the care hitherto exhibited, and if, remembering that they are not yet quite out of the wood, they are careful to avoid, on the one hand, a too lavish expenditure and, on the other, an unwise parsimony, there cannot, I should say, be a doubt that a fair return will, at no very distant date, be made to them on the capital they have expended.

As for the country *per se*, I consider that its success is now assured, whether it remains under the rule of the Company or is received into the fellowship of *bonâ fide* Colonies of the Empire.

In bringing to a conclusion my brief account of the Territory, some notice of its suitability as a residence for Europeans may not be out of place, as bearing on the question of " what are we to do with our boys ?"

I have my own experience of seventeen years' service in Northern Borneo, and the authority of Dr. WALKER, the able Medical Officer of the Government, for saying that in its general effect on the health of Europeans, the climate of British North Borneo, as a whole, compares not unfavourably with that of other tropical countries.

There is no particular " unhealthy season," and Europeans who lead a temperate and active life have little to complain of, except the total absence of any cold season, to relieve the monotony of eternal summer. On the hills of the interior, no doubt, an almost perfect climate could be obtained.

One great drawback to life for Europeans in all tropical places is the fact that it is unwise to keep children out after they have attained the age of seven or eight years, but up to that age the climate appears to agree very well with them and they enjoy an immunity from measles, whooping cough and other infantile diseases. This enforced separation from wife and family is one of the greatest disadvantages in a career in the tropics.

We have not, unfortunately, had much experience as to how the climate of British North Borneo affects English ladies, but, judging from surrounding Colonies, I fear it will be found that they cannot stand it quite so well as the men, owing, no doubt, to their not being able to lead such an active life and to their not having official and business matter to occupy their attention during the greater part of the day, as is the case with their husbands.

Of course, if sufficient care is taken to select a swampy spot, charged with all the elements of fever and miasma, splendidly unhealthy localities can be found in North Borneo, a residence in which would prove fatal to the strongest constitution, and I have also pointed out that on clearing new ground for plantations fever almost inevitably occurs, but, as Dr. WALKER has remarked, the sickness of the newly opened clearings does not last long when ordinary sanitary precautions are duly observed.

At present the only employers of Europeans are the Governing Company, who have a long list of applicants for appointments, the Tobacco Companies, and two Timber Companies. Nearly all the Tobacco Companies at present at work are of foreign nationality and, doubtless, would give the preference to Dutch and German managers and assistants. Until more English Companies are formed, I fear there will be no opening in British North Borneo for many young Englishmen not possessed of capital sufficient to start planting on their own account. It will be remembered that the trade in the natural products of the country is practically in the hands of the Chinese.

Among the other advantages of North Borneo is its entire freedom from the presence of the larger carnivora—the tiger or the panther. Ashore, with the exception of a few poisonous snakes—and during seventeen years' residence I have never heard of a fatal result from a bite—there is no animal which will attack man, but this is far from being the case with the rivers and seas, which, in many places, abound in crocodiles and sharks. The crocodiles are the most dreaded animals, and are found in both fresh and salt water. Cases are not unknown of whole villages being compelled to remove to a distance, owing to the presence of a number of man-eating crocodiles in a particular bend of a river; this happened to the village of Sebongan on the Kinabatangan River, which has been quite abandoned.

Crocodiles in time become very bold and will carry off people bathing on the steps of their houses over the water, and even take them bodily out of their canoes.

At an estate on the island of Daat, I had two men thus carried off out of their boats, at sea, after sunset, in both cases the mutilated bodies being subsequently recovered. The largest crocodile I have seen was one which was washed ashore on an island, dead, and which I found to measure within an inch of twenty feet.

Some natives entertain the theory that a crocodile will not touch you if you are swimming or floating in the water and not holding on to any thing, but this is a theory which I should not care to put practically to the test myself.

There is a native superstition in some parts of the West Coast, to the effect that the washing of a mosquito curtain in a stream is sure to excite the anger of the crocodiles and cause them to become dangerous. So implicit was the belief in this superstition, that the Brunai Government proclaimed it a punishable crime for any person to wash a mosquito curtain in a running stream.

When that Government was succeeded by the Company, this proclamation fell into abeyance, but it unfortunately happened that a woman at Mempakul, availing herself of the laxity of the law in this matter, did actually wash her curtain in a creek, and that very night her husband was seized and carried off by a crocodile while on the steps of his house. Fortunately, an alarm was raised in time, and his friends managed to rescue him, though badly wounded; but the belief in the superstition cannot but have been strengthened by the incident.

Some of the aboriginal natives on the West Coast are keen sportsmen and, in the pursuit of deer and wild pig, employ a curious small dog, which they call *asu*, not making use of the Malay word for dog—*anjing*. The term *asu* is that generally employed by the Javanese, from whose country possibly the dog may have been introduced into Borneo. In Brunai, dogs are called *kuyok*, a term said to be of Sumatran origin.

On the North and East there are large herds of wild cattle said to belong to two species, *Bos Banteng* and *Bos Gaurus* or *Bos Sondaicus*. In the vicinity of Kudat they afford excellent sport, a description of which has been given, in a number of the "Borneo Herald," by Resident G. L. DAVIES, who, in addition to being a skilful manager of the aborigines, is a keen sportsman. The native name for them on the East Coast is *Lissang* or *Seladang*, and on the North, *Tambadau*. In some districts the water buffalo, *Bubalus Buffelus*, has run wild and affords sport.

The deer are of three kinds—the *Rusa* or *Sambur* (*Rusa Aristotelis*,), the *Kijang* or roe, and the *Plandok*, or mousedeer, the latter a delicately shaped little animal, smaller and lighter than the European hare. With the natives it is an emblem of cunning, and there are many short stories illustrating its supposed more than human intelligence. Wild pig, the *Sus barbatus*, a kind distinct from the Indian animal, and, I should say, less ferocious, is a pest all over Borneo, breaking down fences and destroying crops. The jungle is too universal and too thick to allow of pig-sticking from horseback, but good sport can be had, with a spear, on foot, if a good pack of native dogs is got together.

It is on the East Coast only that elephants and rhinoceros, called *Gajah* and *Badak* respectively, are found. The elephant is the same as the Indian one and is fairly abundant; the rhinoceros is *Rhinoceros sumatranus*, and is not so frequently met with.

The elephant in Borneo is a timid animal and, therefore, difficult to come up with in the thick jungle. None have been shot by Europeans so far, but the natives, who can walk through the forest so much more quietly, sometimes shoot them, and dead tusks are also often brought in for sale.

The natives in the East Coast are very few in numbers and on neither coast is there any tribe of professional hunters, or *shikaris*, as in India and Ceylon, so that, although game abounds, there are not, at present, such facilities for Europeans desirous of engaging in sport as in the countries named.*

A little] Malay bear occurs in Borneo, but is not often met with, and is not a formidable animal.

My readers all know that Borneo is the home of the *Orangutan* or *Mias*, as it is called by the natives. N better description of the animal could be desired than that given by WALLACE in his " Malay Archipelago." There is an excellent picture of a young one in the second volume of Dr. GUILLEMARD'S " Cruise of the Marchesa." Another curious monkey, common in mangrove swamps, is the long-nosed ape, or *Pakatan*, which possesses a fleshy probosis some three inches long. It is difficult to tame, and does not live long in captivity.

As in Sumatra, which Borneo much resembles in its fauna and flora, the peacock is absent, and its place taken by the *Argus* pheasant. Other handsome pheasants are the *Fireback* and the *Bulwer* pheasants, the latter so named after Governor Sir HENRY BULWER, who took the first specimen home in 1874. These pheasants do not rise in the jungle and are, therefore, uninteresting to the Borneo sportsman. They are frequently trapped by the natives. There are many kinds of pigeons, which afford good sport. Snipe occur, but not plentifully. Curlew are numerous in some localities, but very wild. The small China quail are abundant on cleared spaces, as also is the painted plover, but cleared spaces in Borneo are somewhat few and far between. So much for sport in the new Colony.

Let me conclude my paper by quoting the motto of the British North Borneo Company—*Pergo et perago*—I under-

---

* Dr. GUILLEMARD in his fascinating book, " The Cruise of the Marchesa," states, that two English officers, both of them well-known sportsmen, devoted four months to big game shooting in British North Borneo and returned to Hongkong entirely unsuccessful. Dr. GUILLEMARD was misinformed. The officers were not more than a week in the country on their way to Hongkong from Singapore and Sarawak, and did not devote their time to sport. Some other of the author's remarks concerning British North Borneo are somewhat incorrect and appear to have been based on information derived from a prejudiced source.

take a thing and go through with it. Dogged persistence has, so far, given the Territory a fair start on its way to prosperity, and the same perseverance will, in time, be assuredly rewarded by complete success.*

W. H. TREACHER.

P.S.—I cannot close this article without expressing my great obligations to Mr. C. V. CREAGH, the present Governor of North Borneo, and to Mr. KINDERSLEY, the Secretary to the Company in London, for information which has been incorporated in these notes.

---

* In 1889, the Company declared their first Dividend.

41

www.ingramcontent.com/pod-product-compliance
Lightning Source LLC
Chambersburg PA
CBHW020257170426
43202CB00008B/403